A WILDER WEDDING

SPECIAL EDITION

A BONUS WILDER ROMANCE

CARRIE ANN RYAN

A Wilder Wedding

By: Carrie Ann Ryan

© 2024 Carrie Ann Ryan

Cover Art by Sweet N Spicy Designs

PRAISE FOR CARRIE ANN RYAN

"Count on Carrie Ann Ryan for emotional, sexy, character driven stories that capture your heart!" – Carly Phillips, NY Times bestselling author

"Carrie Ann Ryan's romances are my newest addiction! The emotion in her books captures me from the very beginning. The hope and healing hold me close until the end. These love stories will simply sweep you away." ~ NYT Bestselling Author Deveny Perry

"Carrie Ann Ryan writes the perfect balance of sweet and heat ensuring every story feeds the soul." - Audrey Carlan, #1 New York Times Bestselling Author

"Carrie Ann Ryan never fails to draw readers in with passion, raw sensuality, and characters that pop off the page. Any book by Carrie Ann is an absolute treat." – New York Times Bestselling Author J. Kenner

"Carrie Ann Ryan knows how to pull your heartstrings and make your pulse pound! Her wonderful Redwood Pack series will draw you in and keep you reading long into the night. I can't wait to see what comes next with the new generation, the Talons. Keep them coming, Carrie Ann!" –Lara Adrian, New York Times bestselling author of CRAVE THE NIGHT

"With snarky humor, sizzling love scenes, and brilliant, imaginative worldbuilding, The Dante's Circle series reads as if Carrie Ann Ryan peeked at my personal wish list!" – NYT Bestselling Author, Larissa Ione

"Carrie Ann Ryan writes sexy shifters in a world full of passionate happily-ever-afters." – *New York Times* Bestselling Author Vivian Arend

"Carrie Ann's books are sexy with characters you can't help but love from page one. They are heat and heart blended to perfection." *New York Times* Bestselling Author Jayne Rylon

Carrie Ann Ryan's books are wickedly funny and deliciously hot, with plenty of twists to keep you guessing. They'll keep you up all night!" USA Today Bestselling Author Cari Quinn

"Once again, Carrie Ann Ryan knocks the Dante's Circle series out of the park. The queen of hot, sexy, enthralling paranormal romance, Carrie Ann is an author not to miss!" *New York Times* bestselling Author Marie Harte

A WILDER WEDDING

The Wilders know their weddings and this time it's for one of their own.

Naomi and Amos have been the secret backbone to the Wilder Brothers' Retreat and Winery for years.

They've also loved and hated each other along the way.

Their on and off again relationship has always worked for them, but now it's getting in the way of the next Wilder Wedding.

If they don't figure out what they want, one of them will have to do what they feared: leave the Wilders.

But if they take that leap, they might just break.

Or finally have what they've always wanted.

Each other.

CHAPTER ONE

Naomi

I loved weddings.

There. I said it. I loved everything that went into a wedding and the day of. Some people called them a spectacle and a waste of money. After all, it was one big party for most people in which money, blood, sweat, tears, and countless spreadsheets went into to make them seemingly perfect. Even though no day was actually perfect.

And I loved it all.

I loved *the moment*. That moment when the bride

and groom, or two grooms, two brides, or any poly mix, found themselves looking at each other for the first time.

I loved the shock, the glee, the terror, the excitement. I loved when brides ended up nearly running to their grooms. Or that one time when the two grooms decided to meet halfway down the aisle, even though it wasn't planned, it just happened. I loved everything about that moment.

The moment you knew that you made the right decision. Where love conquered all and your stomach tightened because you knew this was it. That moment. That everything.

Of course, not all weddings worked perfectly. And not all weddings made sense. Sometimes you went in having a horrible feeling that this just wasn't going to work out. That they were making a mistake with their decisions.

But those didn't happen as often as some people thought.

When you decide to give your all to someone, to promise to love and to protect and to cherish that person, you go all in.

What comes later may change things. Perhaps you're not the same person you once were, so those promises don't mean what they used to. Or perhaps you realize that you were wrong, and you had been looking through rose-colored glasses.

Or perhaps fate deals a cruel blow, and you lose that other person before you even had a chance to make good on that promise.

I sighed and set my chin on my hand as I watched the bride and groom practice their walk down the aisle during the rehearsal. Their wedding was the next morning, and this was a late afternoon rehearsal. Alexis was brand new to the Wilder team, and I was grateful for her and everything she brought not only to the process, but to the Wilders themselves. The past few wedding planners the Wilder brothers hired hadn't been up to scratch. In fact, they had failed so hard I was surprised they could even write a single to-do list.

I had worked here before the Wilder brothers had even come to Texas. To be honest, I had been a little skeptical of them. After all, most of them had no experience with running a winery, running an inn, or dealing with events, let alone weddings.

Six strapping brothers, all in a different state of denial and damage, had shown up at our door and proclaimed themselves our new bosses. Our former boss had decided to retire. He had tried his best, and had laid down a decent foundation, but since the

Wilder brothers had shown up, we had changed for the better.

We were still finding our way, but the Wilder brothers were making things work. And from what I could tell, a few of them were creating sparks of their own.

Alexis and Eli seemed to be enjoying each other's company, although it was my job as innkeeper of the Wilder Inn to ensure that the staff didn't gossip about our big boss and the wedding planner. Nor were we allowed to gossip about our new chef, Kendall Wilder, and her ex-husband, Evan. No, we didn't talk about those things.

Only it was the best thing we talked about.

Sparks flew and one day someone was going to get burned. However, I had a good feeling about them. That meant there were still four more Wilders, and I heard there was even another set of cousins, so there were more sexy Wilders out there. They needed happy ever afters too, and who knew, maybe this Wilder Retreat and Winery could be the thing that changed everything for them.

Because it made changes and hope for others.

It made things spark.

"Excuse me, ma'am? Is this where we check in?"

I immediately turned back to the front of my

desk, smiling wide. I hadn't heard the older couple come in, and that meant I needed to get my head out of the stars and actually focus on my job.

"Yes of course, I'm sorry. Welcome. Mr. and Mrs. Statham, is it?" I asked, remembering their names from the schedule book. We were a large inn with multiple cabins and rooms within our main building, but we weren't so large that I couldn't remember timings and faces if I did my social media scooping well enough. I knew their likes, dislikes, and little touches from the survey they filled out.

Not everyone had social media, so thankfully many people who wanted to enjoy their trip and feel loved and cared for filled out the survey properly. Including allergies, their favorite color, and other random things. The more thorough, the more I could enhance their trip.

I had a whole team to help me with that, to help clean rooms and to keep the large all-wood entryway pristine. But I usually rolled up my sleeves and put in some elbow grease beside them.

Many of the team from before left after our old boss decided to abandon ship. The Wilders had hired so many new faces that sometimes it felt like I was constantly catching up. But the core of us, we were still here.

Like Maddie, Jay, and Amos from the winery. They hadn't wanted to leave the grapes or the barrels, so they stayed, and I had a feeling they would never leave. After all, Elijah and Evan Wilder were kicking ass over there, though I couldn't read Elijah, because I didn't know if he was smirking or not, and Evan liked to growl.

But he fit in over there because Amos loved to growl too.

Not that I was thinking about Amos.

It was better not to think about him. When I had first seen him, I'd swooned.

Yes, I'd swooned.

That big bushy beard and those dark eyes and slanted eyebrows that always made him look angry. I loved them. He was all wide and full of muscle. He could lift like nobody's business, and put some of the Wilders to shame in the muscle department. And when he pushed up his sleeves to his elbows, showing off those forearms? I nearly fanned myself just thinking about it. A girl could weep.

Of course, now I was thinking about Amos while I was checking in our new guests and showing them around the lobby before I led them to their rooms. That was probably bad for business.

Plus, it wasn't great for my heart.

After all, Amos had no idea I had a crush on him. And he didn't need to know—*ever*.

Not only was he older than me, he also didn't like to smile, didn't talk much, and didn't like people. That's why his job at the winery included taking care of the barrels, the machines, and the wine, not dealing with customers.

My job was only dealing with customers. I organized everything on the backend along with Eli and the rest of the Wilders, but I was the first person guests saw when they checked into the inn. Our valet and team out front would welcome them, but half of the time I would meet them out there, welcoming them from their cars.

I loved people, I loved weddings, and I loved the thrill of doing a good job and making sure people were happy.

And Amos liked hiding away and growling at people if they came too near.

I had no idea why I found that sexy. There was something wrong with me.

I got the Stathams settled in their room, and then went back to my to-do list, enjoying the music coming out of the renovated barn. While we called it a barn, it was nothing so rustic. It had once been a working barn, but now it was an elegant ballroom that many weddings and events were held in. Tomorrow it would be all decked out for the wedding. I leaned against the doorway and smiled over at the people laughing and dancing, and one day knew that would be me. Because I believed in happy ever afters. I had to.

It's what I was surrounded by, after all.

And as if my past decided to kick me in the ass, my phone buzzed.

I always had it on me in case of an emergency or if anyone needed me around the inn, so I looked at the readout and swallowed hard.

I didn't want to answer but I didn't have a choice. "Hi, Dennis. How are you doing?"

"You need to come home. Dad needs you. I can't believe that you're spending so much time away when he needs you."

I swallowed the guilt that always came up when I heard my brother's voice. But I wasn't quite sure what I was supposed to say.

"I live three hours away, Dennis. You, Donald, and Dustin all live closer. In the same town. What does Dad need?"

"He just needs help around the house. And that's not our work, that's women's work. You know that. You know you should be home and making sure Dad is safe. It's not like you're out there taking care of a family. You're just working for someone else and leaving your dad in the cold. Just like you always do. So fucking selfish."

I swallowed the lump in my throat, which always happened when I heard from my family.

I was just so tired of not being valued. Of not being seen.

I was the youngest, the only girl, and when Mom died giving birth to me, I became the reason my dad was alone. Something he drunkenly told me enough that I should be used to it.

I was supposed to be the one who stayed home and made sure my dad was sober enough to go to work. To clean up after him. To cook for him. And do the same for my brothers, until they all got married. Somehow my three brothers had found women who could stand them. They all stayed home and cleaned and cooked and were never valued. That was what their husbands wanted, so that's what they did.

And I hated every minute of it. But it wasn't like I could say anything about it. Not again.

I just wanted to be loved. To be valued. To be worth something.

And they had never done that.

"You know that's not happening. Dad has a job.

He has two hands. He can clean up after himself. He's an adult."

"You're such a bitch."

I hung up on him because I knew that no amount of listening to that was going to change anything.

They didn't respect me. And I understood that. I did. But I was just so tired of it.

I slid my phone back in my pocket, and took a deep breath, trying to go back to enjoying the music of the reception, but I couldn't.

"Was that your brother again?"

I whirled at the sound of that deep voice, shame covering my face.

Amos stood there, wearing that sexy Henley and a scowl on his face. He was a full decade older than me and acted as if it were two generations.

Our age difference didn't really bother me. I was in my mid-twenties, he was in his mid-thirties. We worked at the same place. Age was just a number after all. And it was nice being near a man who actually took care of his things, rather than waiting for someone to do it for him.

"It's nothing. I hung up."

"You shouldn't let them talk to you like that."

I rolled my eyes and raised a brow at him. "Really? It's nothing, Amos. I'm used to it."

He scowled and moved forward, cupping my face. I froze, my breath stopping, before I forced myself to swallow. Amos never touched me like this. He was always so good about leaving space between us. About not coming anywhere near me.

But his calloused hand was so warm. It was rough enough that I would love if it touched me more. I couldn't let myself think that because he could always read my face.

His thumb slid across my cheekbone, a raspy sound that sent shivers down my body.

"You need someone to take care of you, Naomi."

"Are you offering?" I asked, surprising myself.

I hadn't meant to say that out loud. We worked together. We were *at* work. And while the bosses didn't care if their employees were together, I didn't need anyone knowing I swooned after a man nobody thought would be right for me.

Amos didn't answer, instead he lowered his head and his mouth brushed mine. I was lost.

Lost, and perhaps finally found.

Three Years Later

"That's it, spread your legs for me. Let me see."

I licked my lips and did as he asked and spread my legs, my hands on my inner thighs as I lay on the bed, my breath coming in pants. Amos had already made me come three times, and I was pretty sure he wanted a fourth. There was no way that was happening.

"Amos. Please. I can't."

"You can. And you will." He leaned down and licked and sucked, nearly sending me over the edge. He pulled away and I frowned, wondering why he stopped.

He licked his lips again and took my thighs in hand. I let out a sharp gasp as he slid deep inside me, stretching me. We had already gone one round, and I couldn't believe he was already ready to go again. Then again, this was Amos. And he was always ready for me. Always knew how to hold me and touch me.

He leaned back so he was on his knees, and I scrambled up him, keeping him deep inside me so I was straddling him, my feet pressed on the bed. And then he gripped my ass and began to lift me up and down his cock. I moved with him, taking his lips with mine.

Tears pricked my eyes, but I ignored them.

It didn't matter that this was everything, that he knew my body so well, I figured he knew it better than I did. He knew how to please me, how to cherish me. He knew how to make me come, how to make me beg.

And he did so again, over and over, and when I came again, he gripped me tightly, arms wrapping around me as he whispered my name, filling me to the point that I knew that I'd be aching afterwards.

I was holding on for dear life for a reason.

Because it had been three years of this. Of stolen nights, of long hours before we could finally see one another.

Three years of watching my friends fall in love, and struggle through heartbreak and happiness.

Three years, where Amos had never told me he loved me.

Three years where I knew he cared for me. That he desired me and wanted me.

Three years where he put me first.

And three years where I loved him more than anything possible but was so afraid to say anything because I knew he would walk away.

Three years where I knew that this could be the end, but I didn't want it to be.

And then Amos was holding me, kissing me, touching me, telling me I was his.

I wanted to say the words, that I loved him, that he was mine.

Only I didn't.

Because I loved happy ever afters. I loved those promises. I loved those vows.

And I had fallen in love with Amos, but I knew the man he was.

And I knew if I didn't walk away first, he would leave me.

So I just held him. And I loved him.

And I waited for the end. Because I was weak for him.

I'd become the person I hated. A person that Amos couldn't love.

CHAPTER TWO

Naomi

P*resent Day*
"Are you sure you're up for it?"

I looked at Aurora and smiled. Aurora was the newest soon-to-be Wilder of the bunch. Since the Wilder brothers had first come to Texas to take over our little retreat that was no longer so little, all six of the original Wilders, and now some of the Wilder cousins, had brought new people into the mix. They were all either married, having babies, or getting married.

Aurora had fallen for Ridge, one of the managers

of the security team that made sure our retreat was safe. And considering what had happened over the past few years, and who actually lived and worked on the retreat now, it was good to have strong support.

And from the way that Aurora smiled just thinking of Ridge, I had a feeling that Ridge supported a few other things than just security.

"Of course, I'm so excited to help. You're getting married!"

I reached out and squeezed her hands, as the baker, cake decorator, and pastry chef of the Wilder Retreat squeezed back. Aurora had been a lovely addition for the entire retreat, and my sweet tooth was grateful that she was here. I had to make sure I didn't go overboard, just like with anything, but I sure as hell knew that I was going to try every single thing that Aurora put in front of me.

"I realize that you helping me taste cake that I make probably isn't the most glamorous way to have a cake tasting for my wedding, but with Ridge on training and assignment, I wanted someone else's opinions."

Aurora's fiancé had left to go train on a new software that would help with security. Trace had wanted to go, but he needed to stay after an incident at the retreat. A not too serious one where paparazzi had gotten in through a downed fence at the back of the property to try to get a glimpse of Bethany Cole. Bethany had married into the Wilders, and was not only an Oscar award-winning actress, she was now a spokesperson and ambassador for UNICEF. And after her recent speech, some people had gotten angry and sent death threats.

We were all used to threats like that, sadly, but things had gotten a little hairy. Ridge had offered to go at the last minute, and had wanted to learn it anyway, but that meant a lot of the planning was up to Aurora now.

"You're telling me I'm allowed to taste cake and enjoy myself? I don't know why you're acting as if this is a hardship."

"I know, I know. I just don't want you to ever feel like I'm taking advantage of the fact that you are our innkeeper and are not allowed to leave."

My stomach tightened at that, but I ignored it. Because I had been here for years now. I started here right out of school and hadn't looked back. I had actually still been in college when I first started working here, and had worked my way up to innkeeper. Which meant I had been here longer than anyone.

I finished my degree before the Wilders had bought the place, and so I had always been in this position, never changing, never moving on. Maybe I should have, but I didn't want to think about that. Didn't want to think about the fact that I felt stagnant, like I was running in place as I tried to come up with what to do next.

Only there wasn't a next.

I was at the top of the food chain in my position. Everything I did wasn't exactly by rote, as the guests were always different, but over time I had pretty much seen and heard everything.

I wasn't sure what I was supposed to do to change things, other than make a huge change that could ruin everything, or maybe make me feel as if I was finally doing something.

"Naomi? Are you okay?"

I smiled and put on a brave face. Because I was fine. Yes, my head hurt, and I felt like maybe I wasn't doing things correctly every day, but I was okay.

I knew that. They knew that.

And if I kept lying to myself, maybe it would become truth.

"Anyway, what cake do you have for me today?"

Aurora studied my face, but I didn't let her look too hard. Everybody knew something was wrong, after all, they knew that I'd had my heart broken. All because I had fallen in love with a man that didn't love me back.

I hadn't realized he didn't love me back. But what was I supposed to do, pretend?

Amos had thought I wasn't old enough to make my own decisions, even though I was nearly thirty. But because he had been an idiot—according to him—who had gotten married as a teenager and hadn't been able to work through his feelings about it before coming to work for the Wilders, marriage itself must be the issue. It didn't matter that he worked at a damn place that hosted more weddings than anything. No, he wasn't good at marriage, and I was far too young. Even though that did not make any sense. But sure, he could break my heart and I could pretend to move on. And we could call it a fucking day.

I was tired of men making choices for me. I wasn't going to let that happen anymore.

I hated that I still loved him and he never told me he loved me. In all those years, he had smiled or had hummed something about him too. But he had never said the words. And that made me an idiot.

I knew that he loved me. I could sense it,

everyone could. But apparently he hadn't wanted me to make the same mistakes his ex-wife had.

Those were the excuses he kept making, and so every time I thought maybe we could work it out, we would just fall apart. Because, frankly, we were not good at this. We should have been, but we really weren't.

"Okay I have three cakes for you to try today, and a few more later. I just want to see what you think."

"You know I love cake. You should go with what you like."

"I know, I know. Ridge picked the groom's cake, which I'm really excited about because it's double chocolate with a praline center. But not the crunchy praline that hurts your teeth, more like a praline cream."

My stomach rumbled. "I hate you right now. Because I really want that."

Aurora winked. "I may have some in the refrigerator for you."

"I take my hatred back. I love you more than I can say."

"Well, that's good to know. I like to have options."

She tapped the three plates in front of her.

"Ridge said that I got to pick this cake because of

course I want to. He wants to make sure I get exactly what I want because he's getting exactly what he wants." She blushed, and I realized that Ridge had not been talking about cake. Well then, I wasn't jealous at all. Okay, I was horribly jealous. Everyone around me was falling in love and finding happiness, and I thought I had been on that track too. Only Amos had decided for us that hadn't been the case.

"Okay, I thought about going with the chocolate and raspberry, but we already have the chocolate, so I'm moving away from that. This one here is a spiced pear with a chai icing. Now if the chai is too much or doesn't work with the pear, I have a brown butter or a cashew frosting instead." My eyes widened, but I took a bite, spices exploding on my tongue.

"That's amazing. Utterly amazing. And I've never had anything like this from you before."

She grinned. "I didn't want just lemon or vanilla. I'll have cupcakes of those flavors on the side for anyone who doesn't like spice."

"Okay, this is already a winner."

She laughed and pointed to the next one. "This is ginger and passion fruit, and I've actually made it as a yogurt cheesecake before, but I wanted to try it like this."

The flavors burst on my tongue, and I had to take a seat, smiling the whole time.

"Okay, what else do you have? Because I'm dying."

"Here we have a coconut mocha. Which is probably too much, but I can't help myself."

I took a bite, the flavors settling deep, and I swallowed, humming to myself.

"This is amazing, but I think the chai might be my favorite."

"Same. Plus, the spiced pear? It's perfect for a fall wedding. Of course, I might throw this all away and go with an almond cake so I could have a lot of fun with the cake decorations. I'm such a huge almond cake fan."

"Whatever you do, have this as one of the cupcakes," I said, pointing to the yummy confection in front of me.

"Then I was thinking maybe go with the almond cake with a sour cream frosting, or just go completely traditional."

"No, you go with what you like. Yes, people love cake, but you go with the cake that makes you excited. You're a baker. Have fun with all the flavors."

"I really love the chai."

"Then have it. And then make the almonds and the lemons and all of the other flavors as cupcakes on the side for those who want them. Because you know you want to make them."

"A cupcake tower might not be trendy anymore, but I still love them. Because I love cupcakes."

My stomach rumbled, and I reached for another bite of the chai cake. "I love all cake. Seriously, you're the best thing that has ever happened to me."

She smiled and winked.

"I would say you're the best thing to happen to me too, but sorry, Ridge beats that." Something flashed over her face, and I knew there was a little regret there.

Because the first time I had really gotten to know Aurora was when Amos and I had broken up for the final time.

The problem was, Amos and I were really good at breaking up. We would get together, and then realize we were looking for different things. The first time was because I wanted fun and happiness, and he wanted heat. And then he decided that this was too much and getting in the way of work, and while I had somewhat agreed, I hadn't realized that breaking up was the way to fix that. And then there was another time when my brothers had shown up and been such assholes that I had been the one to break it off. I was tired of Amos trying to protect me when I knew I could protect myself.

I knew none of it made any sense. Yes, I should just move on. But I had long ago realized that I loved Amos. And he was going to be my undoing.

Aurora and I went over a few other things before I helped her clean up the cakes and I went back to my paperwork. All the guests were checked in and didn't need me for now. Meaning I could finish this up and head home.

Alone.

I lived in the innkeeper's apartment, a place that had been mine for far too long if I was being honest with myself. But I loved the place, I loved how I had made it mine over time.

Though it wasn't really mine. I didn't have to pay for it, it was a perk of my job. I didn't own a home. I didn't have a pet. I wasn't married. I didn't have children. I didn't have all the things I thought I would have at my age. Not that I was aging out of them. It was this being stagnant. Something needed to change, only I wasn't sure what that was going to be.

I finished up my paperwork, humming to myself, thinking that I should probably eat and not just have cake for dinner. Kendall would have something in the kitchen for me, or I could go out. I could even order in. I could probably cook something for myself in my small kitchen, but I wasn't much of a cook. That was something my father had always lamented about.

I frowned, annoyed with myself for thinking about him again.

I did my best not to think of my family. Nothing had changed in the years since I had walked away. They still hated me for leaving and begged me to come back. They still thought I should be at their beck and call, so they didn't have to make any decisions or do anything on their own.

They still tried to bully me into doing what they wanted. I was always the good daughter who came home for Christmas to make sure my father wasn't drinking himself into a puddle.

Which was usually the case.

Annoyed with myself for letting my thoughts wander, I ran my hands over my face and decided to take a walk.

I would let the breeze hit my face, breathe in and out, and then go find something to eat. And then I'd go home—alone—and figure out what to do next.

I hadn't even realized I was walking towards the

vines until I was there. The vines had come with the property, although they had expanded over the years. Between Jay, Amos, Evan, and Elijah, the place thrived. Maddie brought it all together and made sure the wine club and business side were taken care of. But the grapes? Those were Amos's babies.

Before I met Amos, I hadn't realized there was a difference between a grape for chardonnay versus a Riesling. Or that a cab grapes were different too. Or how blends worked. I had no idea what vines did other than you had to take the grapes off the vine in order to make wine. Seriously, the only introduction to wine I had ever had was that old *I Love Lucy* episode. Which apparently wasn't very accurate.

Maybe I would go see Maddie and have a glass of wine. As long as she wasn't too busy with Elijah or the hundred other things that she had on her plate. I loved that so many of the Wilders were here. It was a big family. One I was on the outside of, but still part of. And they never let me forget that I was part of them.

I turned the corner and ran smack into a hard chest. When I placed my hand over his heart to steady myself, he gripped my wrist, not bruising but still firm.

I knew this chest, knew the feel of him. I wanted

to pull away, only I didn't. He looked down at me, a familiar scowl on his face.

"What are you doing out here?" He snapped out the question, a familiar vibe. He was always so angry these days and I never knew if it was just me or everyone that brought this out in him.

I tugged my hand away from him, and thankfully he let me go. Amos was so strong that I wouldn't have been able to break free of him without him releasing me.

That should have been a scary thought, instead it just reminded me of when he would hold my hands over my head and slide into me, long and hard and deep.

I pushed those thoughts from my mind. Those were the past. I wasn't his. Something we were very clear about.

"I'm taking a walk. What are you doing out here?"

"Checking on the grapes. You shouldn't be out here."

"I'm allowed to be here, you know. I'm not going to trample your precious grapes."

"Well, you're lurking. I don't like lurkers."

I rolled my eyes. "What is up your ass right now?"

"Nothing. You just shouldn't be alone."

"Well, that's not my fault, is it?" I snapped, and then could have slapped myself. Really? Did I have to show him that I was still hurting over the breakup? Over our final breakup. Because we were very good at breaking up. Just like we were very good at making up.

"I assumed you'd have moved on by now."

I looked at him, aghast. Had he moved on? My heart twisted, but I quickly stopped it. There was no way I was going to think about that. No way I was going to let myself.

Because Amos falling in love with someone else had never occurred to me.

How had it never occurred to me?

Amos had loved before me but had never told me he loved me. He told me the words hadn't needed to be said.

What a fucking cop-out.

He was going to fall in love with someone else, move on, and I would be left behind. Only I *wouldn't* be left behind. Because I would be right here in the vines with him, having to watch him.

Oh my God, I was going to be sick.

"What's wrong? Are you okay?"

His voice went soft like it always did when he

was trying to care for me, making tears prick the back of my eyes.

How could I be so stupid? He was going to fall in love. He had probably already found someone. Because Amos, despite his asshole-ish ways when it came to communicating, was an amazing person.

He just wasn't my amazing person.

"Naomi?"

"I have to go."

"Let me walk you. Come on. We'll get you to Maddie or something. I'm sure she has some cheese for you. And get you some wine."

"I don't need you to help me, Amos. I don't need you for anything. That was clear the last time we really spoke. You don't need me either."

"What the hell are you going on about?" he asked and looked oddly confused.

"You are the one who broke up with me, Amos. You don't get to act all protective and growly over me."

"And who does?"

"That's none of your concern."

A scowl covered his features as he moved forward, and I held up both hands, keeping him back.

"Stop. Just stop. You wanted it to be over. Well, it clearly is."

I turned suddenly, not wanting to see his face, and ran smack into Eli and Elijah. Both Wilders looked between us, concern etching their features.

And that's when I knew I was a complete idiot.

Here I was, once again fighting with Amos. In public. On work property. While the two bosses watched on.

I didn't know what they were going to say, and I didn't want to hear it. Instead, I just moved past them, running away. I heard Amos call out to me, and I heard Eli tell him that he should just let me go.

And what a crock that was.

Amos had let me go a long time ago.

I just needed to let him go.

I knew exactly what I needed to do to make it happen.

Even if it broke me.

CHAPTER THREE

Amos

I watched as Naomi ran away, and it was all I could do not to follow her. I wanted to hold her close and promise I would never let her go. Only I had fucked up one too many times when it came to Naomi.

First, she had been too young. Then we had been so focused on making sure the Wilders could make it after so many setbacks and other issues, that I hadn't been able to keep her safe. Then finally I realized that all I was doing was making the same mistakes I always did when it came to her. I'd wanted to set her free so she wouldn't be stuck with some guy who was never going to own his own winery, and who would always be stuck working for whoever owned this place, or the next place I showed up at. Naomi still had the rest of her life ahead of her, and I hadn't wanted to hold her back. After all, I had done that before with my ex-wife. I hadn't moved when she needed me to. I hadn't changed my life so she could have exactly what she desired. And while the choices she made hadn't made sense to me, and had blown up in her face, I should have believed in her.

At least, that's what I told myself. My family had all thought that me moving would have been an epic mistake considering that my ex hadn't even had a job in New York. She just wanted to get out of South Texas and move on.

And she had wanted me to go with her, falling into a new life that had never made any sense to me.

I had made the wrong choice for her, just like I kept doing for Naomi.

"Let her go."

I turned to my boss and friend and ran my hands through my hair.

I let it grow out a bit longer this past winter, and I could now put it in a small stubby ponytail if I felt like it. Now it fell over my eyes and I constantly had to push it back. Between that and my bushy beard, I was looking more and more like a mountain man instead of a vineyard manager. It was my job to take care of the vines, as it was Jay's. But Jay was with his family more often than not these days, so I was out of the suits and back into jeans and flannels, keeping our livelihoods safe.

Elijah was the one in the suits now. Though he seemed to always wear them, even while doing quick checks in the vines with me. Somehow the man never got dirt on him, and I wasn't quite sure how he did it.

He was far too spiffy for his own good. Not that I would tell him that. Because you didn't tell Elijah anything. He seemed to know all.

Just like he knew I was once again fucking it up when it came to Naomi.

"I wasn't going to go after her. She clearly wants to be as far away from me as possible."

"And why the hell do you think that is?" Elijah asked, glaring at me.

Eli, the CEO of the company and my other friend, folded his arms across his chest and glared at me. He was very good at glaring. Hell, the entire Wilder family could glare. The brothers, the cousins, the women. I was pretty sure even the kids, once they grew into it, could glare. Although the littlest one had that Wilder pout down pat. It was a little disconcerting when a three-year-old glared at you as if you had stolen their candy. Or perhaps broken their favorite person's heart.

Because everyone loved Naomi.

I loved Naomi.

Not that I had said that out loud.

If I did, I would tether her to me and I would ruin everything.

I couldn't ruin her life.

I needed her to be able to grow, and I couldn't stifle her.

I had loved before, and I'd held her back. And when she left me, I had been the one shattered.

And yet she had been the one to break in the end. So why would I do that to Naomi?

"You know you need to fix this." Elijah moved forward, still scowling.

"I know." I pinched the bridge of my nose, then began to pace down the vines. These were for a Riesling that wouldn't be made for at least another year. We worked our asses off and I loved these vines. I loved every inch of this place. I had put my blood, sweat, and tears into it. Literally in all of those cases.

I had been with these vines longer than the Wilders had, and I felt like I had a claim to them.

But I hadn't left when Joanna had asked. She had wanted a new life but hadn't had any plans for it. I thought we could settle here.

She had hated the word "settle." She thought I hadn't loved her enough to make it work.

"How are you going to fix it?" Eli asked, pulling me from my thoughts once again.

"She hates me."

"You broke her heart. And you know I hate fucking talking about my feelings," Eli grumbled.

I nodded. "I'm pretty sure you and East have a running tally of who hates it more."

Eli's lips quirked for a second before he went back to scowling.

"You win the prize for being an asshole about feelings though," Elijah interjected. "East and Eli here actually do talk to their wives, and sometimes us, about them. But who do you talk to?"

I looked at both of them, confused. "Why the hell should I talk about my feelings?"

"Maybe you should start," Eli snapped.

"I agree with him. Because the more you bottle it up, the more you're going to piss off Naomi. And you're lucky it was just us standing here and not guests. How many times have you two looked at each other and started fighting or walking away or not talking the way that you should in front of guests?"

I flinched as if he had hit me and shook my head. "It's not like that."

"Are you sure? Because it sure as fuck seems like that. You need to fix this. And not just for this job."

The ground fell out from beneath me, and I staggered. "You're going to fire me?"

"That's not what I said," Elijah corrected quickly. "We're not going to fire either one of you. But this place is a family. And I know we all hate when corporate execs say that, but we try to make it that way. Nearly all of our family runs this and works here. And you've been here even longer than we have. This place is a part of you. Just like it is part of Naomi. And we're damned lucky she hasn't moved on to bigger and brighter things. But give her a reason to stay. You have to stop this."

I rubbed my temples before I nodded. "I know."

"How are you going to do that?" Eli asked.

That made me snort. "I have no idea. How am I supposed to fix this when I have no idea where to start?"

"Do you love her?" Elijah asked, his voice so soft it was barely above a whisper.

Elijah had lost the first love of his life in a tragic accident that had rocked this place to its core. Then he had fallen again, and I'd been so damn happy for him. Jealous, but happy.

Both of the men in front of me had found what they needed. They had lives that worked for them and the people they loved.

But how the hell was I supposed to answer him, when I could barely even answer myself?

"I don't deserve her," I answered pitifully. Eli sneered while Elijah just clucked his tongue.

"That's not what I asked. And until you can actually answer that truthfully to yourself, let alone her? You need to think long and hard. Because both of you are our friends and I don't like to see either of you hurt. None of us do. Get your head out of your ass and fix it. Naomi deserves the world. And I thought you were the one to give that to her. Though maybe I was wrong."

The two brothers walked away, leaving me standing alone in the vines, the only thing I had ever been able to be truthful about, and they weren't even mine.

The next day, I knew I had to talk to Naomi. A long night of tossing and turning made me realize I was a fucking idiot. I saw the way the Wilders moved, the way they made things work.

If they could do it, why couldn't I?

I loved her. I fucking loved Naomi. I had for far too long, but I'd been too scared. I needed to fix this.

I wasn't sure exactly how to do that.

I turned the corner, making my way towards the inner workings of the winery, and froze as I saw who was on the tour. Maddie and Jay worked the winery tours, and I would come in for pinch-hitting, but I wasn't the best at it. I didn't like talking to people; I would rather talk to the grapes. In fact, I had a mug from Naomi that said that. I still used it every week and thought of her.

Damn it, I was a lost cause.

Now Maddie was working on a tour and I wasn't sure she even knew who was on it. We had multiple tours through the winery and the vines themselves every day, and I usually steered clear. But I'd been so focused on Naomi that I hadn't paid attention.

And that was my problem.

Because there Joanna was. Why the hell was

she here? I had heard that my ex-wife had moved back to Texas when she had run out of money up in New York. She had wanted to start a small boutique up there, which sounded ridiculous to me. She ran the family small local boutique around here, and it did well enough. It sold local wares, some clothes, and was really for tourists. And people ate it up. We even sent some of the Wilder Retreat guests there if they wanted to go shopping for local things.

But Joanna had wanted to start up something in New York because that sounded like success to her.

That had always been Joanna's problem. Nothing was ever good enough, and she couldn't just settle here. And settling was her least favorite word.

She had settled for me, after all.

Apparently she had come back broke, nearly putting the family out of business, but now they were running strong—and she hadn't come back alone.

I heard she'd gotten married up in New York and brought home the man that she said swept her off her feet. I hadn't spoken to her at all, but her family and my family were still acquaintances. They went to the same church, so they spoke every Sunday, and my mother always got the updates about her former daughter-in-law and her new exploits.

It seemed my mother had been keeping a couple of secrets.

Not just two of them in fact. With a third on the way.

Joanna held the hand of a little boy, while the big man beside her with his clean-shaven face and angled jaw held a little girl. And from the rounded belly on Joanna, it appeared a third was on the way.

I didn't usually see families or pregnant women on winery tours, and that's when I realized this was the full retreat tour, not an actual tasting. Well, there was that. It also meant that they would be seeing the entire retreat, including where Naomi worked.

My blood went cold, because of everybody on this property, Naomi was the only one who knew Joanna.

After all, the two of us had been here the longest, although Naomi had started after Joanna and I had gotten divorced. And the age gap had been one of the reasons I stayed away from Naomi for so long.

It seemed like my past just really wanted to slap me in the face.

"And here's our vineyard manager right here.

Amos, here's some of our tour group; you don't have to say a few words, but you do have to wave. Wave, Amos."

I scowled at Maddie, because I could not believe she was making me do this. I wasn't a fucking circus bear doing tricks. But I waved like the good little circus animal I was, and while most people laughed, waving back, I only had eyes for Joanna.

She looked back at me but didn't look surprised. No, she looked resigned. As if she expected me to still be here. Not moving on, not changing.

"Mother said you were still here. I'm more surprised than I should be."

Maddie looked between us, her eyes widening as she realized that maybe this was awkward after all. She continued discussing the vines and my duties before she gestured everyone to move away.

Joanna and her family didn't.

Instead, they stood there, staring at me, even the little kids. The toddler in the man's arms gave me a weird look and I felt like I was being judged.

Well, that seemed apropos when it came to Joanna's family. Why wouldn't her kids do the same thing?

"Amos?" Maddie asked, her voice low and concerned.

I put on my best fake smile and turned towards Maddie.

"I'll take this crew back to the main room. And then they can meet up with you for the next part of the tour? You're doing the wedding venue next, right?" I asked, scrambling to remember the order of the tour.

Maddie studied my face, looking for answers, but she just nodded.

"Okay. Okay."

She gave Joanna a look that could have been curiosity or condemnation, I didn't know. All I did know was that I was damn glad that Maddie was on my side.

"Joanna. Surprised to see you here."

"I guess I already said that I wasn't surprised to see you here." She cleared her throat. "Jason, darling, this is Amos."

"Nice to meet you," the other man said, but his voice implied the exact opposite.

"This is Rella, Belle, and our Prince Charming is coming soon." She beamed as she said it, and it took me a minute to realize exactly what Rella stood for.

As in Cinderella. Belle, from *Beauty and the Beast*, and the little boy she was carrying was prince charming. I really hoped the kid's name wasn't going to be Prince or Charming. It was hard enough to be a kid these days without a Disney-fied name.

"It's good to meet you," I said to the kids, who just blinked at me.

They were so quiet and well-behaved. It was a little odd considering the only kids that I knew were the Wilders. And the Wilder kids were really well-behaved, but they were anything but quiet. They were kids. They played, they shouted, but they stayed out of the way when they were told. They were respectful, but they were still kids.

These kids looked like pod children.

Or maybe I was just being too harsh. I didn't know them, after all. I didn't know any of them.

"Anyway, we had a free weekend and thought we would come visit and see what the Wilders have done. Things sure have changed since I was last here."

Could this be any more awkward? No, I didn't want to know.

"Well, progress and all that."

"Funny, you didn't really like progress before."

"You know what, let me lead you guys back to the main building," I said, not really in the mood to fight. Because that's all Joanna and I did at the end.

Her husband didn't say a damn thing. He just

looked at me, as if confused how a person like Joanna, all spiffed and polished, would ever want to be with a man like me. I didn't understand either, because I didn't love Joanna anymore. I didn't know why we had clicked in the first place.

But what the hell did I know?

Of course, my own worst nightmares began to come true as a familiar voice sounded from behind me, and I realized Naomi, Wyatt, and Ridge were on their way through, working, but still close enough that they were going to see this tableau.

I really wanted to be anywhere but here.

"Oh, I didn't know you were here," Naomi said, her voice hesitant when she looked at me, and then she looked past me at Joanna, eyes wide. "Joanna."

"Oh, Naomi. You're still here. Interesting."

I moved forward. "Let's get you guys back to the main room."

Naomi just gave me a wry smile that didn't quite reach her eyes. "It's okay, Amos. I can handle this."

"So, the two of you are still together then?" Joanna asked as she looked between us. "My mother loves to talk about the two of you." She looked down at Naomi's hand and smirked. "No ring?"

I could not believe this woman was doing this, especially in front of her kids. I gestured towards the door behind them. "Let's head back to the main room. You don't want to miss the rest of the tour."

Joanna just scoffed. "Okay, Amos. Whatever you say."

"You have a lovely family," Naomi put in, before Ridge cleared his throat, clearly sensing a fight about to brew. Only I didn't know who was going to throw the first punch. Probably the toddler.

"You know what, let me, I'm on my way there anyway. I know Amos has work to do." He gave me a look that spoke volumes before he practically herded Joanna and her family out the door. Joanna smirked over her shoulder again. I hated that look. She was damn good at it.

That left me alone with Wyatt, Naomi, and my own misery.

"Naomi. I'm sorry."

She looked at me before she threw her head back and laughed. "You're such an idiot. I don't care what she thinks about me. She was always a selfish bitch, and now she gets to be a mom on top of it. Good for her. She got exactly what she wanted, but she doesn't get to make me feel like shit. You're the one who always saw her in me." Naomi shook her head before I could speak. "I'm not her."

"I know that. Why the fuck would you think I would ever compare the two of you?"

"Because that's all you did. You were so afraid that you were going to put me in a little box like Joanna said you did to her that you didn't do anything about us. You always pushed me away because you were afraid of what Joanna claimed. But do you notice what I'm saying? You didn't. It was all in Joanna's head. I'm not her. I make my own fucking choices. So, you know what? Keep thinking that I'm her. I'm not. However, I will do one thing that she did, and walk away."

And with that she left, leaving me standing with Wyatt, who looked confused as hell.

"I don't want to talk about it."

The Wilder cousin just shook his head. "I think you just need to man up, grow up, and tell her that you love her."

I glared at the other man. "Pretty rich, coming from you."

Wyatt held up his hands. "We're not talking about me and my own issues. We're really not. But you and Naomi? Fix it. You guys love and hate each other so much, it's very confusing. I don't know what happened between you and your ex, and I don't care. We can talk about it over a beer at my bar, or wine, if that's what you must have."

I laughed despite myself. "You know you like our wine."

"I do, but I digress. Fix this. Just tell her that you love her. Don't do whatever it is your ex thinks you did. Which I don't know what it is, but I have a feeling that a lot of wrongs were made, but probably a lot of rights too. Just, fix it." He slapped me on the back of the shoulder, and headed out, leaving me alone with my thoughts, knowing that I needed to fucking fix this.

Because Naomi was right. And that was the crux of it all.

Joanna had fucked me over and fucked me up, and I seemed to have done the same to Naomi.

It was going to take a lot of groveling to fix this.

A lot of groveling to get her back.

And a lot of groveling for her to actually listen when I told her that I wasn't too much of an idiot.

And I loved her.

Only I had no idea how to even begin doing that.

CHAPTER FOUR

Naomi

I'd made a scene. I could not believe I'd done that. Because no matter what had happened, or what had been said, I shouldn't have. The Wilders didn't deserve it and, honestly, neither did Amos. Yes, I was hurting, and yes, we'd both made mistakes, but I needed to be the bigger person and move on. If he didn't want a future with me, then I would deal. But seeing his ex-wife, and seeing the way that things just spiraled out of control? It made things difficult. And it made me realize that I needed to do better. I needed to figure out exactly what I wanted, and how I was going to make that happen. Because being here, seeing him every day, this wasn't working. I knew that. I needed to stop whatever the hell was going on in my brain.

I would love him until the end of my days, even if I found a way to mute that love.

"Naomi? Why are you standing outside instead of coming in?" Aurora asked as she walked towards the side door of the winery, a frown on her face. I really liked Aurora, and I liked the fact that she made Ridge smile. I hadn't known Ridge as long as I had known the other Wilders, but he and his brothers had moved right on in and had started their lives. Much like their cousins, they came from all walks of life, with different experiences, and were coming together. Although Gabriel, the youngest Wilder, didn't live here because he was on tour currently as a freaking rockstar of all things, he visited often and pitched in where he could. All of them seemed to have this sadness that wouldn't wash away. Not that I was going to let myself think too hard about that considering I was the one standing out here.

Aurora had changed everything for Ridge. She dealt with her own pain in the past, but had come together just like the others had. And now she and

Ridge were about to be married. And I was blessed to call her a friend.

"Sorry, I'm just thinking."

"Do you want to talk about it?"

I shook my head. "No. Not really. Maybe after some wine," I added, when she just raised a brow.

She laughed and we opened the doors, heading into the employee part of the winery.

I loved this part of our routines. It wasn't every week, and sometimes we had to fit it in with small groupings of Wilders rather than everyone, but our girl time wine breaks meant the world to me.

Maddie was the one who usually set them up, and if she couldn't be there, Kendall or Alexis would do it.

It had all started when Kendall and Alexis started to work with the Wilders. While Maddie had been here the longest, the two of us hadn't had wine chats together like this. We clearly had been missing out.

Before the Wilder men had bought this property, and even for the first couple of years after, Maddie and I would meet up when we could, but not like this. It hadn't been wine-tasting, appetizer-devouring, girl time. Where we could talk about our lives and feel like we were a family.

I was going to miss this when I left.

I nearly tripped over my feet as I thought those words. I hadn't let myself think them before. Were they true? Was I going to leave?

Working with Amos day-in and day-out wasn't working. I wasn't moving on. I wasn't figuring out what to do with my life.

I was wallowing, hoping for a better answer to a situation that there were no answers for.

I knew that. I had to.

And that meant I had to leave.

It would break me. Because this was my family now. After all, my own family left much to be desired.

I was an innkeeper. I could work anywhere. And with my experience, I would be able to start at a higher position than I had when I started here as a part-time employee.

I knew this would be different for me.

I could become a manager or do something beyond what I was doing now. I knew if I asked, the Wilders could either help me get in a higher position within their own company, because they didn't just promote within the Wilder family, contrary to popular belief. Or they would give me references and help me find the next step for my career.

I could leave this family, these people that had become mine if I needed to.

Amos couldn't. He was integral to the winery. And while I was integral to the day-to-day aspects of the Wilders, I could be replaced.

I wasn't saying that because I was anything less than him. It was just the nature of our jobs. Replacing Amos would be far more difficult, and it would hurt the business, while I could flourish in other places. Even if it broke me.

I wasn't going to think about that just then. For now, I just wanted to focus on our girl time.

Kendall and Alexis were already inside the employee room, which did not look like any employee break room I had ever seen outside of the Wilders. There were comfortable couches and chairs, and even a beanbag area that I had lain in once after one too many glasses of wine. The ambiance was the same as the front of the house, with luscious wood paneling, a roaring fire, and beautiful decorations. This wasn't just a place to hide a broken toaster and a refrigerator that was never cleaned out. No, this was just as classy and beautiful as anything the Wilders tended to touch these days.

Bethany and Lark were there as well, both in the

small kitchen to the side, organizing the appetizers. I looked over at Kendall who just smiled.

"I wasn't allowed to cook today, so the girls are doing it."

"And we promise not to poison you," Bethany called out, while Lark just laughed.

Maddie came forward, wine in hand, and I went towards her to help.

"Would you like me to pour?"

"Sure, while I explain what we're having today." She leaned over and kissed my cheek.

"It's good to see you."

"Seriously, good to see you," Sidney said as she came around, more wine in her hand. Then she held up a bottle and showed it to all of us.

"This is our non-alcoholic wine. It is not a cider, but something we're trying because we love our mocktails."

"I'm in. All the way in," Alexis said as she clapped her hands.

"It's going to be a long process before we get to the point that we can go on a mass scale, but much like Roy is trying the non-alcoholic beers, and doing really well with them, we're going to try non-alcoholic wines."

"The non-alcoholic gin I tried before was really good," I said as I held out my wine glass.

"Wyatt is having fun with that."

"There's also a mezcal and a bourbon that a few friends are making. I love the fact that if we just want the pretty drinks without all the alcohol side-effects, we can have them."

As Maddie explained the wine we had in our glasses, a beautiful Riesling that I knew would taste amazing, I looked around the room at these women and knew it would break me when I had to leave.

It was time for me to grow, to find something new. I knew that. I felt like I was running in place and had been for a while. Only I didn't want to leave.

I would have to fix this. To change.

Even if I didn't want to at all.

We clinked glasses again, then I took a sip of the crisp pear-like taste of the Riesling. I went back to my beanbag, which thankfully had a structured back so I wasn't leaning too far back, and listened as everyone spoke. I had goat cheese on toasted rounds, and mini quiches that Lark and Bethany had made. They were amazing, but I wasn't going to tell Kendall that.

"I see that look on your faces and these are

fantastic. You can work in my kitchen anytime," Kendall said with a laugh, and I relaxed.

Kendall was not a hothead despite what other people thought, but she was very particular about her food. With good reason.

"Oh thank God," Bethany said as she wiped fake sweat from her brow. "If these didn't work, we were either going to have to raid your kitchen or order takeout."

"Not in this house," Kendall said with a laugh. I ate another bite and hung out with my friends.

"So, how are you feeling, Alexis?" Aurora asked. Alexis had been under the weather for the past few days and was a workaholic like the rest of us. The other woman took a seat next to me in the other beanbag chair. I rested my head on her shoulder, enjoying this time. Was I really going to leave this? No. I didn't have a plan yet. I was just stuck in my head, I would be fine. I had been fine all these years, hadn't I?

And perhaps that was the answer to my own question.

"A little tired. But Eli isn't letting me work any extra hours."

"Damn straight you're not," Lark said, her eyes narrowed.

"I'm fine. Really. You're the one who was sick all last week." Alexis gave her a pointed look and I held back a grin.

Lark blushed. "It wasn't *that*. Though we're not exactly trying, but we're not *not* trying."

Everybody cheered as I tried to do the grammar math in my head, laughing into my wine. At that moment I realized maybe I'd had too much and I set the glass down, annoyed with myself.

I wasn't going to leave these people. They were my friends. My family. My real family sucked.

"And the next wedding is yours, we're getting close," Alexis said as Aurora beamed.

"You mean the next family wedding. I'm pretty sure we have like twenty weddings before that."

"That is true. But yes, the next family wedding. Now we need to just get the other Wilders settled down, and we're eleven for eleven," she said, including the final Wilder who happened to live in Colorado with her family.

"Naomi, you're up," Sidney said, before she winced and looked down at me. "I'm sorry."

I shook my head. "No, don't be sorry. I am the only single one in this room. Which should be more depressing than it is, but I don't know which Wilder is for me. There's the broody one who builds things that doesn't actually ever speak to me," I said, thinking of Brooks. But I knew Brooks had gone through hell and he had a reason for that.

"That is true," Aurora said with a laugh.

"And then there's Gabriel." I let out a dramatic dreamy sigh as the rest laughed. "The voice of an angel who literally is in the news every week with a new woman he's allegedly slept with."

"Never trust the media," Lark said, and I sobered slightly, knowing that the media loved calling Lark a slut even now that she was married.

"I am pretty sure that Gabriel doesn't even know my name, and while I love you guys, I'm not going to marry a Wilder. Sorry, they're the bosses."

"I don't know, it's nice calling my Wilder my boss," Maddie said into her wine, and when we all giggled, she set down her glass. "Perhaps I've had too much to drink."

I snorted again, and listened as they all discussed their plans, and what was coming up at the retreat. Because no matter how much we wanted to have time off and not stress about work, we lived and breathed it.

Another reason why I couldn't leave.

When we all disbanded and cleaned up after

ourselves, I headed towards the main inn, deciding to take a detour through the vines.

I loved walking through here to smell the earth and grapes. It always changed no matter what time of day I went, and it was like a new yet familiar feeling.

When my phone buzzed, I wanted to ignore it, but it could be someone who needed me, or it could be Amos.

No, it wouldn't be him. Why would I think it would be him?

I answered without looking because I had let my mind wander and could have kicked myself.

"Naomi, where do we keep the Band-Aids?"

I closed my eyes at the sound of my brother's voice.

Why was he calling? Why couldn't they just leave me alone?

"Are you at Dad's house?" I asked.

"Where the fuck else would I be? It's not like you're here to take care of him like you should. Like a good daughter would. No, you're making me and my wife do this."

"I'm just going to hang up if you keep talking like that. And why the hell would you think I know where the Band-Aids were? I don't live there."

"But you're the one who organized it last."

Considering it had been nearly nine months since I had been there, I was a little worried about exactly how long it had been since anyone cleaned. My dad was fine. He was just a drunk. He worked and he ate and he drank. That was about it. But he was capable of taking care of himself. He just didn't want to. My brothers were slowly, and sometimes not so slowly, turning into him.

"I put them in the closet on the third shelf from the top when I was there."

My brother began to curse again, grumbling as I heard him walk through the mess of the house and towards the closet.

"Found them. Hell, we only have two left."

"Then buy more." I paused. "Why do you need the Band-Aid? Is everyone okay?"

My brother laughed. "Like you fucking care. You left us. And Dad got a splinter. We took it out, but it's still bleeding."

"Don't let it get infected."

"Like I said, why do you care? We'll take care of it. Nancy's good at it."

I still didn't know what his wife saw in him, but it wasn't my place. It wasn't like they would listen to me anyway.

"Well, just make sure they clean it out, though I suppose Nancy has it."

"Of course she does. She knows family responsibility."

And with that he hung up without a thank you, without letting me know how things were.

Why would I ever want to go back there?

Nobody appreciated me and I was the family doormat.

I promised myself I wouldn't do it again, and while Amos was nothing like my family, he still didn't want me. He didn't love me.

I slid my phone in my pocket, and stopped where I was, closing my eyes to take a breath.

"I am worthy. I deserve to be loved."

And maybe if I kept saying that out loud, somebody would hear me and it would become truth.

I let out another breath, and then fell to my knees as somebody slammed something into my shoulder.

Red-hot pain seared through me and I sucked in a shocked breath, turning to cover my face as another blow came.

And then someone big and bulky was on top of me, pinning my arms above my head.

"What the hell?"

The man slapped me, and it was a man, but I couldn't see his features. He had on a mask, and pinned my arms with one hand, hitting me again with the other, and sat on my hips, keeping me down on the ground. I screamed, kicking my feet.

"Shut up, bitch. Shut up. I'll show you what you've been missing. Do you think you can look at me like that and get away with this? You've been teasing me. Moving those hips like you want me to fuck you, and then leaving me bone dry? Fuck that. I'm going to make sure you remember exactly who you are and who you belong to."

Alarm shot through me, and I kicked, screaming again as he hovered over me, glaring through the mask. I didn't know what this man wanted from me other than the fear running through me. I didn't know *how* he knew me or what I'd done inadvertently to catch his attention. But he knew me. And he wanted to hurt me.

And I couldn't get away.

Someone had to hear me. The vines weren't that big. Someone had to be out here.

"Stop, stop!"

Then the man was pulled back off me and I rolled to my knees, shaking as I stood up.

"Amos!" I called out as I ran towards him. He

had the other man down on the ground, but then Amos fell back. The other man got back to his feet and began to run through the vines, and I realized that he had tased him. Just a small taser, not ones with the prongs or anything like that, but enough that Amos had been shocked back, and hit the ground.

I ran to him, ignoring the man, and cupped his face.

"Are you okay?"

Amos cursed and cupped my bruised cheek. I flinched, and so did he. "Are *you* okay? Baby. He hurt you."

And then as the others came running, asking what had happened, I fell into his arms, shaking, and let the tears come.

Because I had just been attacked in my own home, in my own vines.

And yet seeing Amos on the ground like that?

It had put more fear into me than anything.

And I had no words for that. None at all.

CHAPTER FIVE

Amos

Rage poured into me so violently that I thought I was going to scream. I couldn't get the sound of Naomi's shouts out of my mind. I knew they would echo forever in perpetuity, taking away my soul ounce by ounce. Nor could I get the sight of that man pinning her to the ground out of my soul. It would always be there. But she was in my arms now, shaking as she cried.

My Naomi. She rarely cried. Though sometimes it felt like that was all she was doing around me these days, because I was such a fucking asshole, but I'd be damned if I would let this hurt her. I couldn't.

I just held her, crushing her close, even though I wanted to run after the asshole who would dare hurt her. All I knew was if I let her go, that would be the end of this. I couldn't let her out of my arms. I had to make sure she was safe. Which meant I had to let someone else do the running.

Trace and Ridge came through the vines as three other security team members went in the direction that the attacker had run. They must have seen this on the cameras we had over the vines. They had seen this but hadn't been close enough to stop it.

Just like I hadn't been close enough until it was nearly too late.

I had done my best to keep her safe but it wasn't good enough.

None of it was fucking good enough.

"I've got you, baby. I've got you."

She just clung to my shirt, her fingers digging in as she began to calm down.

Only there was nothing calm about me.

"Amos. We're here. Naomi?"

She froze at the sound of Trace's voice, as if coming out of a trance.

And then she moved back, her tears drying on those pale cheeks of hers. She had such fair skin, delicate skin. And she had a red mark on her face. One I was sure would turn into a bruise soon.

That man had dared put his hands on her. I knew I would see similar marks on her wrists. I wasn't sure I could look. If I did, I would run towards the man and rip his face off. No matter where he went, I would find him and end him.

I hadn't realized I would kill for someone before, but I would do it.

"Baby, your face."

She frowned up at me, her hand going to her cheek, before letting it fall.

We didn't say anything, just looked at each other, and I wasn't sure what there was to say.

"I'm fine," she muttered, before she scrambled off my lap and to her feet. She staggered back, as if her legs were weak, and nearly fell into Ridge, who reached out and gripped her elbows to support her. Part of me wanted to growl, to step forward and pull her out of his arms. To yell at him for daring touch her.

Naomi wasn't mine. And me being a territorial asshole wasn't going to help any of this. Even though it felt like it was the only thing I could do in this moment.

"Naomi, you're okay. You are okay, right?" Trace asked, using his best calm voice.

"I'm fine. But Amos was tased."

I was already up on my feet and scowled at her.

"It was barely anything, I'm fine."

Trace cursed under his breath as he took a step closer, but I held up my hand. Yes, my hip was going to be sore later, but the damn thing had mostly surprised me. That was the reason I had let go off the man. Of course, I would have let him go to check on her anyway. Because my mental wires were fried and I needed to make sure that she was unhurt. Only that hadn't been the case. That bastard had marked her. Had put his hands on her.

I was going to kill him.

"Either way, the authorities and the EMTs are on their way."

She shook her head quickly, and I cursed again, knowing what was coming. Because that was Naomi, just as bullheaded as me. It was why we never got along and yet fit so well together. Why I fucking loved her and needed to tell her that. But now wasn't the time.

"I don't need anything. I'm fine. No broken bones. No cuts. I'll be a little sore, but I just want to go home, okay? I just want to forget this ever happened." She rubbed her hands over her face, but winced when she touched her cheek. My eyes narrowed and I moved forward, grateful when Ridge took a step back. When she opened her eyes and looked at me, I glared at her.

"Either you come with me up to my apartment over the barn back there, or you wait for the EMTs. You're not going to get a choice in this."

"Since when do you make my choices for me?" she asked, and this was an echo of our past conversation, though it didn't make it any easier to deal with.

"You get to make the choice. I'm just giving you the options."

"I'm fine."

But she was anything but fine, just like I was.

"Naomi."

Ridge and Trace didn't say anything, although I knew they were keeping an eye on our surroundings. I didn't know where that man had gone, or who he was, but we were going to find out. First though? I was going to make sure Naomi was safe.

"Fine. Your apartment. Then I'm going home."

"You're still going to have to talk to the authorities," Trace put in. "But before that, do you know who it was? Did you see his face? We couldn't see anything on the screens."

Naomi blanched, and I realized that she must not have heard him mention the cameras before, and she hadn't thought of them.

"You saw. Hell. Of course, you saw. Because we try to keep this place safe, and someone just attacked me." She shook her head. "I don't know who it was. He was wearing a mask. I didn't recognize his voice. But the way he talked? It was like he knew me. He knew my name. But that's all I could think while..." She rubbed her unhurt cheek and sighed. "I just want to get out of here, okay? I'll talk to whoever I need to. But I just need to get out of here and sit down."

Before we could go anywhere however, the authorities arrived, and she went over what happened in detail. The team hadn't been able to find the attacker, nor had the authorities, though they were still canvassing the retreat. Trace had a good relationship with them so they were all working together to figure out who had done this. They'd asked Naomi question after question about what had happened or who she thought could have done this. When they'd mentioned ex boyfriends, she'd only mentioned me, but as I'd been the one to pull the man off her, I didn't seem to be a suspect, but I'd answered their questions as well.

So many fucking questions and yet there were no answers. She'd waved off the EMTs who had scowled. But since I'd worked with one of them before I'd worked the vines, they'd taken my word that I'd bring her in if there was an issue. Not exactly by the book, but nothing felt like it was these days. I was so fucking tired of people hurting my friends, and I'd be damned if I let anything else happen to Naomi, but I wasn't sure what else I could do except make sure she was safe in my arms.

They said a few more things, and then I was leading her away from the vines and towards the barn. I had lived in that two-bedroom apartment above the barn since before the Wilders had bought the place. Yes, they had upgraded it since, but this was my place. It came with the job, and I was grateful for it. I didn't see myself moving anywhere else. Actually, the only time I'd ever thought about moving at all was when Naomi and I had been getting serious.

We were silent on our way back to my place. I

knew her mind had to be going a thousand different directions, because honestly mine was doing the same. Although I wasn't sure what we were supposed to say to each other. There were no right answers. There was no way to make this work. But we had to. I just didn't know what to say. I had fucked up so many times. And not being with her right then? Not making sure she was safe? Perhaps that was the worst thing I had done. Or at least the worst recently.

"Come on, let's get you cleaned up." I cleared my throat as we made our way upstairs. "You left a pair of your leggings and a top here so you can change."

She looked at me and frowned. "And you kept it?"

I sighed and then moved her back into the kitchen. When I lifted her up by her waist, she didn't stop me. She just looked at me, confused, as I set her on my small kitchen island and went for my first aid kit.

"I didn't know how to give it back to you. You know I'm not good with goodbyes. Not good with talking. Sometimes I feel like I'm not good at anything."

"I don't know if I quite believe that," she said after a moment.

"What do you mean?"

"I think that you're good at a lot of things, Amos. I was actually thinking about that today. Before…"

"They'll figure out who it is, Naomi. They have cameras everywhere. We'll see who the guy is, or our teams will catch them. They're good at this. I'm just fucking pissed that anyone got to you at all."

"It's a hundred acres. I can't really give the man an excuse, but I'm so fucking annoyed that it happened."

I ran a washcloth under the sink and began wiping the dirt from her face, anger riding me hard as I did.

"He hurt you." I gently wiped her cheek, and she didn't flinch. She stared at me, and I sighed.

"Naomi. How hurt are you?"

She looked down between us, and I realized she had her wrists out. There were red marks on them, and I knew she would bruise, just like she would on her cheek.

"I'm going to kill him."

"Don't. They're going to catch whoever it is, and then they'll deal with it. You don't have to, Amos."

I cupped her unharmed cheek and set the washcloth beside her. "I'm always going to worry about you, Naomi."

When she moved her hands, I froze, letting her decide what was going to happen. Letting her decide because I hadn't before.

She slid her hands through my hair, and then over my beard, as if studying me for the first time.

I swallowed hard. She smiled softly and I leaned down, doing the one thing I shouldn't.

I brushed my lips against hers, and she sighed into me.

"I don't want to hurt you," I whispered.

"Just, kiss me? I just want you to kiss me. And to touch me. Where it's not him."

I understood that clear as day. Because I didn't want to think about that man touching her either. So I kissed her.

My hand slid down her shoulder, over her arm, down to her wrist. When my thumb slid across the delicate skin there, she didn't flinch. Instead, she pulled back slightly and met my gaze.

"I'm not fragile, Amos."

"You sure as fuck feel breakable to me. You're so small. So tiny in my arms."

"And you were there. Thank you. I'm sorry I didn't say that before." She frowned before I could say anything and started pulling at my shirt.

"What is it? What do you want, baby?" I asked, her motions frantic.

"I need to see. Where he hurt you."

"Okay. I'll help." I used my free hand to pull my shirt over my head and tossed it to the side.

"See? I'm just going to have a bruise on my side. It's just a bruise. He didn't hurt me. It was more startling than painful."

"He could have hurt you more. He could have hurt you so much. And you were just there to protect me."

"And I'll be there, Naomi. I don't regret that for an instant."

"He hurt you."

I cursed under my breath, and then I took her mouth again, needing her taste, her touch. Her hands slid up my chest, her nails digging into my skin until she wrapped her arms around my waist, bringing me closer. I was cradled between her legs, her ass on the edge of the kitchen counter.

"Take me to your room?"

Her voice was so soft, and I knew she was being gentle for me. Because she was so damn afraid. But hell, I was just as afraid.

So I didn't let myself think. I didn't let either one

of us speak. I just lifted her into my arms and carried her away.

"I've got you."

This movement was similar to before, so fucking familiar. Because I had held her like this. I had touched her and needed her, and then the two of us had made love on every inch of this apartment. But had I called it that before? Had I told her anything? No. I had let my emotions and my actions be enough. Only that was never the case.

You could pretend it was, but it wasn't. Not when you were breaking deep inside and the other person couldn't read your fucking thoughts.

I needed to be better. Needed to tell her what I was thinking. Even if I had no idea what that was.

I set her on the bed and then I gently pulled down her leggings, taking her panties with them.

She lifted her arms as I took off her shirt and undid the clasp between her breasts. The bra fell, and I leaned down and sucked one rose-colored nipple in my mouth, then the other. Her breasts were small, but still filled my hands. Just the perfect size. She was the perfect size for me. As if we had been made for each other and I had been too fucking stubborn to let myself believe that.

"Tell me to stop, Naomi. I don't want to hurt you. Not with everything that just happened."

"Just stop talking for a minute. Please? I want your touch. Not his."

She kept repeating that and I swallowed hard before kissing her again and continuing to make my way down her body. I cupped her breasts between my hands, letting myself take my fill as she slid her hands through my hair. I knew she liked the rough of my beard against her skin. But it would leave marks. Just like the marks that fucking man had made. But these weren't the same. She wanted this as much as I did. This wasn't like before. This wasn't like anything. This felt familiar, as if we had been here countless times in ages past, and yet I was thinking clear. Maybe she thought I wasn't, but I was. Because I wanted this. I craved this.

I kept kissing down her body, over to her wrists, gently pressing my lips against the red marks that would bruise. And when I kept kissing down her stomach, she arched into me. I pressed a kiss to each hip bone, licking my way along the creases.

She moaned as I spread her thighs and finally took a look at the center of her.

She was so beautiful. So wet and flushed.

I had tasted her before, had her coming on my

tongue and on my hand and in every position possible. And yet this felt like the first time all over again.

It was funny. I couldn't remember the last time we had been together. Because it hadn't felt like a last time then. It had just felt like an every time. And maybe that was the problem. That we had taken for granted what we had. No, that was me. I was the one who had done that. And I was going to fix this. I knew I had to. And I would find a way to do that. But first, I needed her.

I lowered my head and began to kiss her, slowly, leisurely, spreading her lips as my tongue darted in and out of her pussy.

"Amos," she whispered, rocking onto my face. I slid one finger deep inside her, then a second; she was so tight, and I knew soon I would be deep inside her, needing more of her.

But first I needed her to come, needed her to flush pretty pink all the way to those nipples as she writhed on my hand and my face. She tasted of sweet honey and everything I loved about her.

I wanted her to be mine. Only I had been too cowardly, too chickenshit to realize it in time.

I continued to kiss her until she was coming, whispering my name, and I knew she was back in the past with me.

We weren't thinking of the future, weren't thinking of the disastrous mistake we were possibly making.

But it didn't matter, it was all I could do not to slide into her right then.

I had to be careful, I had to take my time with her. Something I hadn't done enough of before.

As she lay there, still coming down from her orgasm, I quickly stripped out of the rest of my clothes and slid a condom on.

And then, before I hovered over her, I remembered.

She might not want me on top with everything that had happened. I slid onto my back and rolled her over me.

"Ride me. You make the choice. Always you, Naomi."

Her eyes opened wide for an instant, as if realizing, before she swallowed hard and nodded. But instead of straddling me, she pulled me up to a sitting position.

"Together," she whispered, and I wiped away a tear along her cheek, hating myself, but needing her in that moment more than ever before.

When she slid over me, both of us crying out in pleasure, her inner walls tightened around my cock.

I held her close, my hand tangled in the back of her hair, her hands holding my shoulders.

And then we were moving, meeting thrust for thrust, need for need.

This didn't feel real, and yet it felt like everything.

I would hate myself in the morning, but for now I would show her that I loved her.

Show her that I could be hers. Just like she could be mine.

But she didn't say anything, instead she just met my gaze before closing her eyes and throwing her head back, pushing her breasts towards me. I sucked on one nipple then the other, and then she was coming, tightening around my cock, and I moved harder, faster. And when I followed her, I held her close, burying my head against her neck, whispering her name.

Whispering the words she had never heard before, but I knew she couldn't hear now.

I had almost lost her. More than once.

I held her as we both came down and hoped she wouldn't think this was a mistake. That she wouldn't walk away like I had before.

Only I had a feeling that I wasn't that lucky.

I had broken her.

And I didn't know how to put her back together again.

So I just held her.

And once again I let myself pretend. In the morning, no matter what happened, I would find the man who hurt her and I would break him. And then I would break myself.

After all, it was what I deserved.

CHAPTER SIX

Naomi

There are moments in life when you realize that you had clung to something because you were scared, that mistakes didn't just start with the letter m, but with the big fat capital letter M.

As Amos sat there, with me on his lap, I realized that this was one of those times.

I was such an idiot. Yes, I had been scared, yes, I had needed someone to hold me, but I hadn't needed to do what we had just done. We were both consenting adults, but I had lost my damn mind when it came to him. But then again, wasn't that always the case? It was why I clung to him now. Because I was that idiot. Always.

"Are you okay?"

I nearly laughed. What an absurd question to a traumatic and yet even more absurd day.

Because he wasn't meaning to make me feel like I had made a mistake. No. He was just doing what he did. Taking care of me, but not taking care of himself.

Because maybe if he had done that, maybe if he had tried to do that so long ago, I wouldn't be falling into a million pieces.

"I should clean up. The others might check on us soon, and things could get awkward."

He frowned, then pushed my hair back from my face. Such a casual gesture, such a familiar one. He was forever touching me, trying to keep me calm, to keep me in his hold.

He had never hurt me like that. But I had never truly known if he was mine. And perhaps that was a kind of hurt after all.

"Okay. Let's do that."

I smiled as I climbed off him, the feeling of loss once he wasn't inside me annoying, but something I was used to by now.

I hated the fact that I loved him. But that was on me. Not him.

I went to the restroom and cleaned myself up before pulling on the clothes that he had set out for me. My own clothes that I had left here, like a forgotten memory. Like pieces of me that I didn't want to know again.

I felt like there was something truly wrong with me, but it had nothing to do with him.

I stood day-in and day-out watching people vow to each other that they would be with one another forever. And somehow knew that was never going to be me.

I had been attacked. Hurt. But I knew they would find out who it was. That we would find answers. Because there wasn't another option. The Wilders protected their own.

Amos had gotten dressed at the same time as me, and I swallowed hard as I looked at him, at the concern on his face.

But he didn't say anything.

And I shouldn't have been shocked.

"Can I get you something to eat? You should be resting." Amos ran his hands through his hair and then cursed under his breath.

"Did I hurt you again? You should have been

resting, not me being a fucking neanderthal and taking you like I did."

I let him speak, rambling about how I needed to be cared for, how I needed to rest. And I knew if I didn't leave right now, I wouldn't. And I would be stuck in the same cycle as before.

With a man who cared for me. But didn't see a future.

Because if he had, he would've said something before now.

"We can't do that again."

He paused in his ramblings right as I spoke, then frowned. "Of course not. You were hurt. Come on, let's go rest. And you're right, one of the Wilders will probably show up any minute to make sure you're safe. Hell, I turned on the security alarm when we walked in, but I need to double-check it."

My heart ached, because I knew he was trying so damn hard. But I was tired.

I loved him so much and this was going to break me. But it would be worth it. For both of us.

"We can't do that again because I'm never going to hate you, Amos. And that's the problem."

He froze in the act of looking at the alarm before turning towards me. "What are you talking about, Naomi?"

In that moment I saw all our months together, our years. He had always been there, taking care of me, but would push me away when things got to be too much. Because I was too young for him, or was too much like his ex. Or maybe that's just what I told myself because I needed to believe there was a reason he didn't want to be with me.

I was stronger than this.

"I can't do this again because I will never hate you. How can I hate you, Amos? I love you."

I said the words I had told myself I would never say aloud, and his eyes widened in surprise.

How could he be surprised? After so many years of me wanting him, he looked fucking surprised.

"Amos? If we keep doing this, if I keep letting myself fall, I won't hate you. I'll hate myself. And I don't know how to fix that." I paused, and yet he didn't say anything. He didn't tell me that he loved me too. That he wanted to be with me forever. He let me speak. Which he always did. But I needed him to say something. And when he didn't, I finally continued, "I'm going to leave. I can find a job anywhere. The Wilders said that Roy's team could use me."

His eyes narrowed at that, but I didn't let him ask why I would know that. Because I had spoken to Eli about this. Not this exact situation, but when he had given me my last raise, we talked about my future. And when I mentioned something possibly outside of the Wilders, he had looked hurt but was also my boss. We were friends, all of us, but the Wilders were my employers. So they knew there was life for me outside of here. And Roy's team needed a new innkeeper and executive manager. That could be me. It should be me. Because Amos needed to be here, and I couldn't be near him anymore.

"Naomi."

I shook my head. "No. I'm going to go. Right now, and probably for good. Because I can't love you anymore. It's killing me to love you. And I can't try to hate you anymore. It's not worth it for either of us."

I moved past him and went to the door.

"Naomi."

"What can you say to make me stay, Amos? Anything you say will just make it worse. Thank you for saving me. Thank you for being there when I needed you. But this is so unhealthy for both of us. And I don't want to hate you," I repeated.

I opened the door to see Ridge standing there, and I wanted to cry. Why was he there? Had Amos asked him to get me to leave? Or was Amos letting me leave so easily because he didn't want me there?

I pushed those thoughts out of my mind because they didn't matter. This was on me. This was my choice. And I was going to be the one who did this. Not him, not anyone else.

This was on me.

"Hey. Sorry I'm interrupting."

Ridge's gaze took in my disheveled hair and new clothes, then looked over Amos, and raised a brow. But the man didn't say anything. Good, because I didn't want to break down right there. I was pretty sure I would any minute.

"We were just having a conversation," Amos said, as if willing Ridge to leave.

I cleared my throat. I didn't want to hear what Amos had to say. I didn't want him to tell me that he cared for me, that he wanted to still be friends, that I didn't have to go. Because we had done this before. We had tried the friend thing, and it never worked.

I loved him too much for this.

I needed to love myself enough to go.

"Can you walk me back to my apartment? Do you mind?"

"No problem. I don't have an update for you on anything, but we're staying vigilant. Everyone else is safe," he added, and the relief that I hadn't realized I'd been aching for slid through me.

"That's good." I swallowed hard, the tears threatening to break. "Thank you for telling me. Can we go?"

"Of course." He looked over my shoulder at Amos. "Lock the doors behind us. Keep your alarm set."

"Yeah." Amos was silent for so long I thought that would be it. That he was just going to let me go and everything would just fall into place with me not being there. So I didn't look back at him. I took a step towards Ridge on the outer deck, when Amos finally spoke.

"Naomi, we'll talk in the morning, okay? Once you get some rest. We'll talk."

I didn't look at him, my hands shaking in front of me as a tear began to slide down my cheek.

Ridge frowned at me before looking over at Amos. I knew the two men were probably questioning each other with looks, but they didn't say anything. I was so glad that they didn't ask me anything else. I didn't answer Amos, because I knew us speaking wouldn't lead to anything.

I loved him.

He wouldn't tell me he loved me.

So I was going to move on.

Something I should have done a long time ago.

Ridge walked me towards a golf cart, and as he drove me towards the main inn, I let the tears fall but I didn't make a sound. I wiped at my cheeks, grateful that Ridge didn't ask me anything. He was good for situations like this. He was growly and contained and exactly what I needed.

Someone who wouldn't ask me what was wrong.

Maybe he would think this was because of the attack, and maybe the adrenaline finally wearing off was part of it, but that wasn't it. Not in its entirety.

Alexis stood in the doorway, Eli at her side as we pulled up, and while I didn't want to speak to anyone, I was glad to not be alone.

And wasn't that something. I was waiting for everyone else in their couple form to take care of me.

Because I couldn't seem to take care of myself.

"Let's get you tucked into bed, shall we?" Alexis asked, but she didn't ask me why I looked like I had shattered into a million pieces.

Couldn't everyone see those shards of glass on the ground? Those parts of me that I was leaving behind with every step?

Couldn't they see that I wasn't the Naomi I needed to be? That I was the Naomi I had become due to my own actions. My own inactions.

I didn't say anything as Alexis and I walked into my rooms and she closed the door behind me. I knew she said something to Eli, probably something about the kids, I didn't know. It was all I could do to wipe my cheeks, and then realize that I wasn't keeping up with the tears.

"Let go. I've got you," Alexis whispered, and then I was in her arms, kneeling on the ground, as sobs wracked me.

Because it wasn't just embarrassment and anger and pain radiating through me.

It was everything.

I cried in my friend's arms, with the family that I had made, knowing that I was going to have to walk away again.

Because nothing had been fixed. And this might finally be the true ending that I hadn't realized I was waiting for.

This was my ever after.

But there didn't seem to be anything happy about it.

CHAPTER SEVEN

Naomi

"Thank you so much for being here. I hope you enjoyed your stay." I smiled at the older couple as they waved their goodbyes and practically skipped towards the valet.

I let out a soft sigh, that feeling of accomplishment settling in.

Despite the fact that I was ready to give my notice and leave, I loved this job. I loved working with these people, and I loved making people's days.

I loved working with the Wilders, and figuring

out new and innovative ways to make sure people knew that they were welcome here.

And I liked making sure that the Wilder Retreat became and remained a success.

I was a critical part of that, but I was also replaceable.

So after my shift, I would head to Eli's office and have the meeting I had been postponing for far too long.

I was still a little sore from the attack, and the Wilders and Trace never let me out of their sight these days, since they hadn't found the man who attacked me, however, I was okay.

Heartbroken and shattered, but resilient.

Which had taken far too long for me to realize I needed to be.

I hated this so much. I wanted to stay. Even though I knew I needed to grow, I wanted to remain. But I had glorious references, and I knew the Wilders would help me no matter what. And I would find a job that wanted me and cared for me just as much as the Wilders.

I held back a snort at that, walking back into the lobby to make sure everybody had what they needed. I wasn't sure I would ever find something exactly like I had with the Wilders. That would be too difficult. Especially when they had become my family.

It would hurt to leave, but I needed this. For my career, and for my heart.

I was not running away. Maybe if I kept telling myself that, I would believe that, but I was not running away.

Damn it.

"Naomi, you're here."

I turned and smiled at Aurora, the woman looking radiant as always.

It might have had something to do with her wedding in two days, or it could have just been the fact that Aurora always looked happy lately. I didn't think it was only because of Ridge. She had grown so much since she made the decision to move out here. She'd started over and found a new life and a family she adored.

And while our situations were vastly different, I couldn't help but think about the fact that she had changed. Had moved on.

I knew I needed to do something similar, although our paths were so different it wasn't even funny. I didn't want to leave them. I wanted things to work out.

"Are you okay?" Aurora asked, pulling me out of my thoughts.

"Sorry, I'm fine. Just going through my checklist for the day. How are you?"

"I'm great. I wanted to thank you again for the cake help. Ridge is excited about cake."

I laughed at that, shaking my head. "I can't wait for the wedding. And the cake."

"It's going to be so much fun. And I love that Ridge and I aren't having anyone stand up for us." She blushed. "Not that it wouldn't be amazing to have fifty people on either side of us, but I like that it's just us making our promises to each other, in front of our family and friends."

I felt as if my face would crack from how hard I was smiling. Because while I was so happy for her, so enraptured in the fact that she was finally getting her happy ever after, I was jealous.

And that was a problem. I didn't want to be jealous anymore.

So I wouldn't be. I was going to grow up and figure out exactly what I needed to do with my life. Because wallowing over a man I couldn't have wasn't it.

"I can't wait to see you in your dress. You're going to look amazing."

She blushed, shaking her head. "It's odd, shopping for a second wedding dress. Especially because the first one brought me here."

I smiled at that memory, that what she had done must have been the hardest thing, but she made another bride happy, and I had introduced her to Ridge. It had ended exactly how it should have, even if it had taken heartbreak and tragedy to bring them there.

"Well, I also have a new dress, just for the occasion." I shrugged. "All of my friends keep getting married, and I like to wear a different dress each time. It's a tradition."

Thankfully I wasn't the bridesmaid in all of these, or I was going to actually end up like the girl from *27 Dresses*. This time I could wear the dress I wanted, even though it was never going to be a wedding dress.

And that was something I needed to not spiral over. I needed to get over this and be fine. There was nothing wrong with me. I just was in the dumps a bit.

"Anyway, I was headed towards Signature to work with Kendall tonight."

Signature was the high-end restaurant we had at

the property, and while I could not afford to go there without my employee discount, I loved it.

"Oh, are you working there tonight?"

"I'm just helping the pastry chef for a bit, because they have a large party, and I'm not allowed to work on any wedding cakes other than my own right now, and I'm on schedule."

I beamed at that. "Because you're the next wedding."

She did a little dance in her heels. "And I'm the next wedding," she repeated. "But I did want to ask you if you had the contact information for the couple for when I get back? It wasn't in my files."

It hit me then that if things worked out well, I wouldn't be here for that wedding. Aurora and Ridge were going to be taking some time off for their honeymoon, but when they came back, they would jump right back into it.

And if I went to Eli and gave my notice and actually went to work for Roy or someone else, I wouldn't be here for that wedding. This was smart. I would be able to go into a new position, to grow, and to problem-solve. I wouldn't have to look my past in the face every single day.

"Yes, I do. Let me get that for you."

"Awesome. Thank you. I guess with everything going on, I didn't get all the information I needed."

"It's why we're all here. Because we work well together."

"It's the perfect team." Aurora gave me a quick hug before she walked away, leaving me feeling like I was making a wrong decision.

I wasn't. I couldn't be.

Ridge came by a few minutes later to check on me, and then Trace, and then more from the security team.

I hated that they needed to be here. That we hadn't caught the man that hurt me. It was someone who knew my name, who wanted to hurt me, and while I felt fear and anxiety over it, I was trying not to let it control everything that I did.

Which wasn't easy.

"Hey, Adam?" I asked one of Trace's men.

"What's up, Naomi? You need help?"

"No, but I do have a meeting with Eli."

A meeting that would change everything if I let it. But this was important. I knew it was. This was what I needed to do. It would be better for everyone.

I kept repeating that and I knew I needed to stop. To get out of my own head.

"I'll walk you up there."

"We're inside. It's just right up the stairs."

Adam gave me a look. "And you really think that Amos is going to like it if I let you walk up there alone?"

I frowned, annoyed. "I don't really think Amos has any say over what I do. Do you?"

The other man winced. "I'm sorry. How about this, do you think Ridge and Trace would like it if I let you walk around on your own when we don't know what's going on? They're my bosses. They could fire me. You wouldn't want that on your conscience, would you?" That made me roll my eyes.

"Fine. Fine. Do what you have to."

He grinned at me and we made our way up the stairs, talking about the upcoming work meeting, when the lights went out in the hall.

I nearly tripped up the stairs but he gripped my arm, catching me before I fell.

"What was that?" The only light was coming in through a window further down the hall.

"Not sure. We'll get upstairs. Probably a breaker?"

"Sure." I let out a weak laugh. "Totally. That's it." But the emergency lights hadn't come on and that was a problem. We had drills for power issues and the emergency lights *always* lit up right after the initial power went out. We'd have to get someone on that as it was a potentially dangerous situation for our guests.

He frowned at me and I opened my mouth to say something but was cut short. I let out a scream as someone tugged my hair and Adam let out a strangled sound. The sound of a taser going off again sounded in my ears as Adam hit the ground but kicked out as he went down. I turned, the hallway too dark to see who was coming at me, but the guy pulled my hair again and I fell down two steps, hitting my already bruised hip.

"You think you can run away from me? Fuck you. You think these little security guys can help you? I'm just as good as they are."

I knew that voice. And not just as the man who attacked before, though yes it was him—I realized this was Morgan.

One of the wine club leaders who was here every week with Maddie. Who talked to me and asked about my day.

Morgan, the former special ops guy who was just as trained as anybody on the security detail.

Alarm spread through me as I slipped in blood trying to go up the stairs and I realized it was Adam's blood.

My eyes had finally adjusted to the darkness, and I looked to see Adam lying across the stairs, blood seeping from a head wound that Morgan must have given him.

I scrambled up the stairs, trying to get away.

"You think you can just smile at me and lead me on? I saw the way you've been with Amos, that asshole. He's nothing compared to me. But I know you wanted him.

"You think you can just walk away like I meant nothing? If you were truly with Amos, if you truly loved him, then you would be with him. You should have just been with me. And then I would never have had to hurt you."

He hovered over me, and I didn't dare move. Not with the taser in his hands still, not with the way that he looked at me.

I barely remembered this man; I had barely spoken to him. I just wanted to get out of here.

But he'd hurt Adam. I could see Adam's chest rise and fall, so I knew he was still alive, but I didn't know anything beyond that.

"You're going to come with me. You're going to walk to my car, and then we're going to get away from this. I'll protect you. You won't need the

Wilders anymore. You won't need any of this. You're just going to need me."

My hands shook, but I wasn't sure what to do, what to say to get out of this. I wasn't sure I could say anything to get out of this.

"Morgan."

His whole face brightened. "You see? I knew you'd remember me. You remember my name. Everything about me. We were always meant to be, Naomi. Always."

He leaned down to try to press his lips to mine and I flinched. I didn't mean to; I didn't know what else to do. But when he glared at me, I knew I had done the wrong thing. He lifted his hand, either to smack me, or something else, I wasn't sure, so I leaned away, knowing I couldn't get out from under him like this.

I could kick him, I could slash out, but he could hurt Adam or me more.

And I wasn't sure what to do.

But then he was being pulled off me as footsteps thundered around us, and I was pulled into strong arms. Arms I knew. Arms that I loved.

Amos held me close, as Trace and Ridge and the others went to Adam and Morgan, dealing with them.

"It was the wine club guy. The guy who was always so nice. The guy who I thought had a crush on Maddie. I didn't do anything. Promise. Oh my God. It was Morgan. It was Morgan."

I kept repeating it as Amos held me close, carrying me up the stairs and into the workroom next to Eli's office.

He ran his hands over me, checking me for injuries, and I just stood there shaking.

"Did he hurt you? Naomi? What happened?"

I shook my head. "He didn't hurt me. I fell and I bruised myself probably, but he hurt Adam. Adam was bleeding." That's when I realized I had blood on my hands, on my sides.

Tears began to fall in earnest, and Amos cursed under his breath.

"Baby, is any of this yours?"

I shook my head. "It's Adam's."

"The others will make sure Adam is taken care of. But I need to make sure you're okay."

"I'm fine. I'm fine."

I began to calm down and tried to come to terms with what had just happened. I pulled away from Amos, knowing I needed to be strong.

Because I wanted to break down in his arms, but I couldn't.

Not when we would just fall back into that same cycle. And I couldn't. Even with everything that was going on, I could not get back into that cycle.

"You should go check on them." I gestured behind him towards Trace, who stood in the doorway, looking us both over. "Trace is here. You should go back to work or something."

He scowled at me. "I can't, Naomi." He paused, his gaze bracing. "I love you."

I wiped away the tears, telling myself I would not cry again. "You can't say you love me when the world is ending, Amos. You have to say it in the good times. Not just the painful. How can I know you mean it?"

He cursed under his breath. "Of course I mean it, Naomi. You didn't let me tell you before."

"You mean the last time I was attacked? Amos, I can't keep doing this."

"I mean it. I love you."

But before I could say anything, before I could tell him to go, or to fall in his arms at the words that I had been waiting to hear forever, the authorities and EMTs were there pulling us away, and I looked across the long hall at him, wanting him to stay, needing him to leave.

Knowing I needed to make a decision.

Because I had waited forever to hear those words.

I was afraid it was too late.

That he would push me away again when the cloud of losing me would fade away.

And I had to be worth more than that.

Or maybe I could have everything I had ever dreamed of.

I hated not having the answer.

CHAPTER EIGHT

Amos

The next morning it was all I could do not to sit outside of Naomi's place and make sure she was safe. But that would put me into stalker territory, and I already hated myself enough. I didn't need to add any felonies or misdemeanors.

When the authorities had pulled us from each other so they could check on her and ask us questions, it took all my self-control not to bundle her up in my arms and take her with me. To never let her go.

But I also wasn't going to be the man who forced her to stay, not after what that asshole Morgan had done. I still couldn't believe that had happened. That a man had taken it into his own hands to try taking Naomi from us.

Her scream would once again echo in my dreams until the end of time. But she was safe. Adam had a mild concussion and needed two stitches on his forehead but was fine. He was more angry with himself than anything, but I told him it wasn't his fault. After all, it was the asshole Morgan who had done it. Adam had put his body and life on the line to protect the woman that I loved. I owed him everything.

Even if Adam thought differently.

The next Wilder wedding was the next day, and I knew there were a thousand little things we needed to do to make sure we were prepared. We were not going to let a thing like assault and a threatened kidnapping affect Ridge and Aurora's wedding. They had already been through enough hell. They didn't need to have this in their way. So after I finished with my duties at the winery that morning, I was helping set up.

I hadn't seen Naomi yet, but I would soon. She would be at the wedding, and I would have to hold back so she didn't hate me. But I needed her to know that I loved her.

I needed her to believe me. It was on me that she hadn't. After all, I hadn't said the words because I had been too chickenshit before.

I had let my relationship with my ex affect me, and I wasn't going to do it again. The fact that my ex wasn't even part of my vernacular these days told me I was over her. But I had been too damn scared, and I wasn't going to let that happen again.

"Hey, Amos? Can we talk for a second?"

I turned to see Eli standing there, the big man scowling a bit, but it didn't look like it was directed at me. At least I hoped to hell it wasn't directed at me.

If anything, he looked contemplative and a little worried. And that set me on edge.

"What's up Eli?"

"It's about Naomi."

I stepped forward, my palms sweaty. "Is she okay? Did that asshole get out of jail? Where is she? Is she safe?"

Eli held up both hands. "I'm sorry. I should have prefaced by saying she's fine. In fact, I just finished speaking with her in my office. And that's why I'm here."

Dread pooled in my gut, and I didn't want to hear what he had to say, but I knew I didn't have a choice.

"She's fine. But she was on her way to me yesterday for a meeting where she was going to give me her notice."

The floor beneath me quaked and I held on to the railing to keep from falling over.

"She's leaving?"

"You can't be surprised, can you? She wants to try new things. And she wants to be happy. I know the two of you need to talk, need to work through things. Or you need to let her go. I'm already having to hold Alexis back from kicking your ass because we don't want to lose Naomi."

"I'm already kicking my ass enough for both of us."

Eli shook his head. "Not enough. Fix this. Because we can find a way for Naomi to build a future here. If she doesn't want to be the innkeeper anymore, but wants more responsibility? She can do whatever she wants. We will find a position for her that works. Because she's family. And I'm going to tell her that. But if she needs to leave because of you?" Eli shrugged. "Then we're going to have a problem."

"I'll go. She doesn't need to. This is her home. Her family."

I knew the way her brothers were, the way her father was. I knew all of that. There was no way that I was going to let her leave the family she had made to start all over again. She didn't fucking deserve that.

No, I loved her. And I needed to prove it to her. I needed her to stay.

And that was what I would do. I would walk away. I hoped to hell she would stay.

"You're family too, Amos. Just fix it, okay? I don't know what's going on between the two of you, but let's just work through it. Don't make me get involved."

And with that, Eli walked away. I let out a deep breath before I followed him towards Naomi's place. I hopped in the golf cart and drove the distance there, telling myself that this trip felt far longer than it should have.

We had lived near each other, had been with each other, had worked together for years, and yet I hadn't been enough for her.

Why did I keep thinking that she was waiting for the next step, waiting for something better to come along?

I was such a fucking idiot.

I needed to prove that to her. Prove that I was worth her—she already knew I was an idiot.

I pulled up to the inn and noticed Alexis and Aurora glaring at me. Aurora was getting married the next day, and here she was, scowling at me.

Well, I fucking deserved that.

I walked past them and didn't stop. I knew if I did, they'd threaten me, and while I would deserve it, I needed to get to Naomi first.

You would think after all these years I would have come up with a plan. But, of course, I hadn't. I was just standing outside her door, knocking and hoping something would come to me in time.

She opened the door to her small apartment and frowned.

"Amos? What's wrong?"

I had forgotten that we had a party to go to tonight. The rehearsal had already come and gone a few days ago, as everybody had been preparing for a few other weddings, so tonight was just a small get-together with everybody who lived and worked here, and Naomi was already dressed for it. She had on a dove-gray top with leather leggings, leggings that I had bought for her last Christmas because she hadn't wanted to buy them for herself.

She had mentioned wanting them in passing when we had been sitting in my living room, each scrolling on our phones, but would never have bought herself. So I had taken note and looked over her shoulder to see what she wanted, and got them for her.

I hadn't even thought twice about it. Because she made me fucking happy.

And yet I pushed her away. Why? Because I was a dumbass. That was why.

"Everyone's fine. I just wanted to see you. You look gorgeous. You know I love these pants."

She frowned for a moment, blushing slightly. "Is it weird that I think about you every time I put them on?"

"That was sort of the point," I said truthfully. "Can I talk to you a moment? If you want me to go, I'll go, but the thing is, I've been running for far too long, I'm either dragging you along or leaving you behind in the process. All because I was in my own head, afraid that I was going to force you into something that you didn't want. Force you into whatever our lives could have been."

She stared at me a moment before she took a step back, and I realized she was barefoot, her toes painted the same silver as her top.

I swallowed and stepped in, following her as she closed the door behind us.

"I'm not your ex-wife. I never would've blamed you if we had tried and failed, but we never tried. And that's on me, too, you know." She threw her hands up in the air. "I never told you I loved you."

"You did."

She frowned. "What?"

"You would whisper it in your sleep, and I'd whisper it back, but I was too cowardly to actually say it when you were awake. I didn't want to take away your choices. I love you. I have always loved you, Naomi. But I failed you." She didn't say anything, so I continued, hoping I wasn't making too much of a fool of myself.

"I'll go with you. If you leave here because you want to spread your wings and find a new job, if you let me, I'll go with you. I can find work anywhere."

"But these are your grapes. Your vines."

"They're the Wilders' vines. I love taking care of them. I love having my hand and stake in something that people enjoy, something I'm good at. But I can start over too. There are so many fucking places that I could work. Places we could work together. But if you want to leave? To go and leave me behind? I'll hate that. I'll hate myself for letting you go, but I won't make that decision for you. Because all I've done is make decisions for you."

"Amos."

"I'll let you walk away, but I'll fight for you first. Because I love you, Naomi. I love being with you, I love laughing with you. I love watching these Wilders make so many fucking mistakes and yet become the best possible people they can, while I'm standing by your side. I want to watch you grow. And I want to grow with you. So let me love you, Naomi. And let me prove to you day-in and day-out that I do."

I hadn't realized I moved forward, cupping her face until I was wiping away her tears and she had her hand on my chest. But she wasn't pushing me away. She just held on, a sigh escaping her lips.

"I just wanted you to fight for me."

"I'll always fight for you. Not with you. I love you."

I lowered my head and took her lips with mine.

She sank into me, and we both groaned. I just held her, *needing* to hold her.

Knowing I could have lost everything without even knowing I had it in my hands.

"I promise I'll never take this for granted again."

"Same. I should have told you. Just like you

should have told me. Maybe if we weren't so lost in our heads, afraid of what could have happened, we would have been here together long before this."

"We had to wait for the Wilders to get their heads on first. Now we're following suit."

"I don't want to go. I don't want to leave my family."

"Same. So we'll stay. We'll figure out the next phases together. Because I love you. And I love watching these Wilders have these weddings with you." I laughed at our familiar refrain before I kissed her again and she sank into me, mine. Always.

This moment had always been on the brink. We'd always been the ones on the sidelines, the backbone of this retreat.

And we had lost so much time, but we wouldn't lose anymore.

"I'm going to spend the rest of my days proving I'm worthy."

"As long as you let me do the same," she whispered, and I held her, and knew that the days weren't going to be easy. We would make mistakes, and we would still have to deal with the trauma of everything that had happened.

But in the end, it didn't matter.

The only thing that did was me holding her in my arms.

I finally realized what I should have long ago.

That I loved her, and I needed her.

We needed each other. Every step in every way.

Even if we fought along the way. Because the making up was always the best part.

CHAPTER NINE

Naomi

A Wilder wedding was full of cake, wine, spirits, and cheese. Of course, I figured the cheese had to do with the Montgomerys that were visiting thanks to Ridge's cousin Eliza.

Amos had his arms around me, and I leaned against him, feeling like I was coming home for the first time in a long while. Eli met my gaze across the dance floor and I smiled at him. Because after our talk that morning, even though none of us were supposed to be working, I knew that I *was* home.

I wouldn't be going off to spread my wings anywhere else, instead I would do that right here. With my family, and without having to deal with moving.

I didn't know how much longer I would be the innkeeper of the Wilder Retreat, but soon I would be moving into an executive position. They needed me and they trusted me. And I would hire and train my replacement.

That meant I could finally have a place of my own outside of the retreat, and Amos would be right there with me.

While it had taken us years to get to this point, everything now was coming at a fast pace.

I was getting not only a promotion, but I'd be finding a home with the love of my life.

There was no going back now.

"Your mind is going a thousand miles per hour," Amos whispered before he kissed my neck.

I'd been so afraid that he was going to leave me behind, I hadn't realized I'd been doing it as well.

Maybe if we had just told each other what we wanted, it wouldn't have been like this. We wouldn't have wasted so much time. Or maybe this was the time we needed. To figure out exactly what we wanted.

But here we were, changing everything. And I loved him.

"Bride and groom seem happy."

Amos mumbled behind me, kissing the other side of my neck.

Everybody looked so happy as they went out to the dance floor to join the happy couple.

Eli and Alexis twirled, their daughter between them. Their other child was with the nanny, still too young to be at a wedding like this.

Evan and Kendall danced together near the side, their children in the corner with some of the other kids. Everett and Bethany laughed as he twirled her around, with Lark and East joining in. Maddie and Elijah only had eyes for each other as they danced past us.

Sidney and Elliot danced slowly together, while Trace forced Wyatt into a dance. Wyatt just rolled his eyes and leaned his head dramatically on Trace's shoulder, until Elliot scowled and forced Sidney and Trace to trade places. And then Elliot was the one leaning his head on his husband's shoulder while Wyatt twirled Sidney.

I laughed, loving the camaraderie of it.

Brooks stood off in the corner, watching it all,

and I didn't blame him. Today had to be hard for him for many reasons.

And Gabriel, fashionably late as always, stood up on the stage, crooning a tune that made my eyes sting.

The family was growing by leaps and bounds, and they had not only loved us enough to let us stay, but trusted us to become part of their family. They had gone through hell and back, each and every one of them, and they were here, fighting for a happiness they all deserved.

And we did too.

When Amos pulled me onto the dance floor again, I leaned onto his chest, hearing his heart beat against my ear.

"We're getting better at dancing," he whispered.

"I only stepped on your toes a few times that first time."

"True. But we're better than the rest."

I smiled up at him. "Probably because we have the most experience."

"Because I love dancing with you in the fields, under the moonlight."

My heart swelled, and I realized that this was it.

We wouldn't be breaking again.

I had finally found my family, and he had finally learned to settle into his.

We didn't need to run from the choices we were afraid to make.

When Alexis and Elliot called out for all the single women to stand in the center, I glared because there weren't that many of us left, just me and the children and a few other adults. Only when I caught the bouquet, the others laughing with me, I just looked at Amos and raised a brow.

"Well, I'll see what I can do." He winked as he said it, and I threw my arms around him.

"I like working on our own timetable. Even if we're both a little afraid of it."

"Just a little," he whispered, pressing his lips to mine.

"Hey you two, part ways for just a minute," Eli said, and I raised a brow at him even as Amos didn't let me go.

"What do you want, Wilder?" Amos growled.

"Well, it might be the wine talking, but you know I realize that both of you might have wanted to leave the retreat for reasons other than personal."

Alexis sighed beside him. "He's not firing you. I promise. But, we might be buckling at the seams of this retreat one day, because we keep building on the land, so if Wilder Wines and other parts of our business decide to franchise, we just wanted to make sure you knew that you were both honorary Wilders. Just saying."

I blinked at them, before throwing my head back and laughing. "And here I was, worried that I didn't have a place."

"And here I was worried that she was going to want to make new choices, turns out you guys are the ones making them for us."

Alexis scowled when Eli grinned this time.

"I am the puppet master. And you will do as I say."

"Sure, baby, whatever you say," Alexis said with a laugh.

"I like being an honorary Wilder," I said softly. "Although, Naomi Wilder? I don't know, I don't think it has the right ring to it."

Amos chuckled beside me. "It better not," he grumbled, and then he was kissing me again, and everyone was laughing and dancing, and I knew that this Wilder wedding was one for the books.

It wasn't the first, nor was it going to be the last. There were a few more Wilders to go, and if Alexis and the others had anything to say about it, they would get them exactly who they needed when the time came.

But I only had eyes for Amos.

The man I had been so afraid to lose, that I never really let myself have in the first place.

I loved him with every ounce of my soul, and now he was fully mine.

Heart, soul, body, and future.

And while we still had a lot to work through, a lot of stress to deal with, a lot of changes to make, I knew that no matter what happened, I finally had a choice in the matter.

And my choice would always be Amos.

For now and forever, no matter what vows we make.

BONUS EPILOGUE

Amos

Why was I nervous? Oh yes, that was why I was nervous.

I ignored my thoughts and went back to work, kneeling on the ground, my hands in dirt and soil and nutrients and everything that went into the vines, and inhaled deeply.

It was a crisp morning in South Texas, so that meant as soon as I inhaled, I sneezed, moving my head towards my elbow as I did.

Evan chuckled roughly beside me, standing as he looked off into the distance, over the land that his family owned.

I was never going to be a landowner like this; I

was never going to own my own vines and winery. And that was damn fine with me. The amount of work and frustrations I saw just by watching the Wilders work meant that it was not something that was in the cards for me. But being in charge of certain vines and knowing that the Wilder wine brand was becoming something synonymous with quality and expertise, meant I was doing a damn good job where I was.

"You know that mountain cedar is hitting hard. Why are you taking such deep breaths outdoors?"

I stood up and wiped my hands on my work pants and glared at my boss and friend.

"I was trying to enjoy the morning and really get to know the grapes. But apparently allergies are a bitch even when you're on two allergy medications."

"You know, I never had allergies when I lived outside of Texas. Even when I was stationed in Virginia and my buddy always had huge eye issues thanks to the pollen there, mine was just normal. Yes, sometimes I had to take a twenty-four-hour non-drowsy med, but it's not like the prescription allergy meds that I am on out here."

"I'm thinking about doing the shots. Just to see if that will help."

"Eli did that, and his throat still gets scratchy

during cedar season. I'm pretty sure cedar season is just hell for everyone involved."

I shook my head and looked over the grapes again, smiling just a little bit at the look of them. The vines were fucking beautiful, and I loved my job, even with the allergies.

"At least grapes don't get allergies like humans do."

Evan quickly spit over his shoulder and glared at me, so I did the same and we each spun around counterclockwise.

"I can't believe you just made me do that."

"I can't believe Jay has us both doing this. I don't fucking believe in superstitions."

"You're a retired military guy who works with wine. You are a superstitious man."

"Okay, that's fair."

I grinned, and we made our way back to the main building of the winery. I knew there were a few tours going on and Maddie and Elijah would be busy. Later that night the Wilders would all be meeting over at Wyatt's place. I knew he had a few things going on that were urgent, which meant Wilder attention was going to be on that rather than the winery, and I was fine with that. He wasn't my direct boss, but he was a friend now. And he needed us.

That always gave me a kick in the pants, that the winery and the distillery would be forever vying for who was the number one distributor on the property.

And yet I had a feeling that Alexis and Eli with their wedding business were probably going to win. Of course, East's work with the spa was just increasing that, since it was all copacetic and worked together symbiotically.

"So you think we're going to beat Wyatt this year?"

"Yes."

I looked over at Evan, who shrugged. "This year. Next year? We'll see. They're newer, but we're in a mixed cocktail era."

"Well, good thing we're mixing wine into the cocktails now. And not just sangria."

"We're taking over the world." Evan cleared his throat and gave me a look as we walked inside. "Speaking of taking over the world. You ready for this?"

I scowled at my friend. "I shouldn't have told you anything. Now you'll just glare at me if I'm not doing it quickly enough."

"Because you've made me keep a secret from my wife, and that means I'm going to have to kick your ass."

"I don't know how, because she can always read you." Although I did feel slightly bad about that. After all, the deed should have been done last week, but then an emergency had sprung up, and Naomi had needed to leave the property. Then we hadn't had time to deal with anything, so that meant today was the day.

If everything worked out.

And if she finally fucking answered me.

"So you didn't have to ask her father for permission, right?"

I snorted. "Fuck, no. The only person that is allowed to answer is her. She's the one who gives herself permission. Her family isn't worth shit."

And while that made me sad to think about, considering what she had grown up with, she had made her own family with the Wilders, just like I had. And we would be each other's family, as soon as I got down on one knee and finally asked her to be my wife. I was only a couple of years late doing so.

I was going to finally ask.

Finally make sure that she understood that we were each other's forevers.

"It'll be nice to have another wedding here. I swear we don't do enough of those."

I laughed at the dryness of his tone. "Well, I guess we will be next *if* she says yes." I pulled at my collar as Evan laughed.

"She's going to say yes. And then we have two more Wilders to go."

"That's not on me. But I'm sure Naomi and the girls have plans."

Evan raised a brow. "Really?"

"Well, they always seem like they're running the world. So I assumed that they have plans for this."

"Honestly, you're probably right. But Brooks and Gabriel should have what we have. And you know that this family loves fucking weddings."

"And what are you going to do when you run out of Wilders?"

Evan just shrugged. "I'm sure there're other family members out there that need it. Or hell, another family connected to us."

"I guess that makes sense. I'm going to head into my meeting, and then I'm going to try not to freak the fuck out."

"Good luck with that. But we both know you're going to fail." Evan held up both hands. "At not freaking out. Everything else is going to work out though. I promise."

"So says the man who married the same woman twice."

"I made the right decision twice, I just happened to make a fucking wrong decision once, but I fixed that. And I'm fixing it and repenting every fucking day."

I laughed and headed to my meeting, knowing that today was going to be a long ass day.

By the time I finished my meeting, and one emergency after another, I wasn't sure that everything was going to work out like I want it to.

We were already ten minutes late heading to the distillery for the family get-together, and while we weren't exactly family in name, we were close enough.

"Why are you all fidgety?" Naomi asked, her arm wrapped around my waist.

I had my arm around her shoulders and cleared my throat.

"Just hate being late."

"True, but I'm always early to things, and you're the one who's always late. So I'm not quite sure why you're suddenly worried about that." She frowned.

"Are you sure you're okay? I know your allergies are bothering you."

Fucking cedar.

"I'm really fine. Sorry. Just losing my mind a bit."

We had stopped then, standing on one of the stone steps that went from the main section towards the second barn where some of the weddings were held. We were heading towards another golf cart so we could make our way to the distillery on the other side of the compound.

The place was so big that you could drive it in a regular car and not feel like you're wasting too much gas. And while sometimes we walked it, my girl wore a sexy as fuck dress that went down to her knees before flaring out, and high heels. I loved it when she wore high heels.

"You look beautiful."

She smiled up at me, her eyes warm. "Thank you. You clean up quite nicely yourself. I love how long your beard's getting." She reached out and tugged on it gently and I leaned down, pressing my forehead to hers.

"I had a plan you know."

Her hand fell and she moved back, looking up at me. "For today? I know you had a bunch of emergencies. I'm sorry."

"You can't really stop it when life gets in the way."

"I know. But we're on our way now. And we're only a little late. And knowing the Wilders, we're probably not the only ones."

I nodded, my breath coming a little faster, stress starting to seep in.

I dealt with a multimillion-dollar company every single day, and yet right then I was so damn nervous. There was probably something wrong with me, but I couldn't think past this moment—the woman in front of me, the woman that I had fallen in love with long before I'd gotten the courage to say it.

"Did you know the first time I saw you, I knew there was something special about you?"

"Really? I think the first time you saw me, I was bent over a toilet trying to get it unclogged." She shuddered. "I really do not miss those days with the old bosses."

I smiled, remembering that day.

"True. But you were such a spitfire, and were damned annoyed at the asshole boss we had."

"At least he wasn't our main boss."

"True. That guy was a nice old man who tried

his best, but didn't really know how to hire management."

"But then we got the Wilders. And they do an okay job."

"Yeah, okay."

I winked, nerves wracking me.

I could do this. I had thought about doing this for far too long. Now I needed to just get up off my ass and do it.

"And I know it took me a long time to get here. To get out of my head and realize what I had been missing all these years."

She smiled softly, but then I think she really understood what was about to happen because her eyes widened and they began to glisten just a bit.

I had to be fast or I wasn't going to be able to get this out.

Which meant that I had to actually say the words.

"I'm so damn sorry that it took so long. That we lost so much time. But I love you, Naomi. I love who you are, and who you make me. I love watching you strategize and figure things out. I love you working hard for everyone around you, making sure they have the best. I love the way you make me feel, and the way I know you will always be there for those that you love. I love the family you have made, the family *we* have made." I swallowed.

"Amos."

"Let me finish or I'm going to fuck this up more than I already have."

She let out a watery laugh and nodded, smiling so bright I knew that this was what we both deserved. Even though she deserved it long before now. "I can't wait to make more of a family with you. And I can't wait for you to see who we can become. I'm sorry I was so blind to it before, that I was too fucking afraid. But I love you. And I want you to be my wife, Naomi. I want to get married here, in our home, with our family. I love you, Naomi." I went to my knee, my hand shaking. "Marry me. Be my wife. And let me be your husband. Marry me and let me continue to be the happiest fucking person in the world."

Tears streamed down her face as I pulled out the old-fashioned ring that had been in my family for generations. It was a diamond surrounded by other diamonds, but had pearls woven in. It wasn't new or up-and-coming. It was a little ancient, a little worn, and yet I hoped it spoke to her.

"It's so beautiful. This is your grandmother's ring."

I nodded. "She would've wanted it for you. We're making a new family here, and we'll have some of the old, the family that we want together."

"Yes. Yes, I'll marry you. I love you so much, Amos. And I'm so glad that we finally got our shit together."

I laughed at that, both of her hands shaking as I slid the ring on her finger. And then I was standing, my mouth on hers, as I claimed the woman that I loved for all to see.

Because, of course, we weren't alone.

The Wilders stood around us, cheering and clapping. I wondered why we were all late, but then I looked at Evan and narrowed my gaze at the other man.

"Sorry. I lied."

"Like my husband could ever keep a secret from me," Kendall said with a laugh. And then Maddie and Elijah were opening champagne, and under the lights, the stars of Texas, the stars of San Antonio, and the fairy lights of the Wilders', I toasted to my future bride as our family, the Wilders and more, surrounded us.

"Here's to another Wilder wedding," Eli said, holding up his glass. Naomi laughed, and I joined in.

Because we weren't Wilders by birth or by marriage. But we were Wilders by soul.

And in the end, weddings were what they did best.

While I was late to the party, I wouldn't be late to this.

I held Naomi close and toasted to our future.

And the countless days to come.

ALSO FROM CARRIE ANN RYAN

The Montgomery Ink Legacy Series:

The Wilder Brothers Series:

The Montgomery Ink: Boulder Series:

Book 1: Wrapped in Ink

Book 2: Sated in Ink

Book 3: Embraced in Ink

Book 3: Moments in Ink

Book 4: Seduced in Ink

Book 4.5: Captured in Ink

Book 4.7: Inked Fantasy

Book 4.8: A Very Montgomery Christmas

Montgomery Ink: Colorado Springs

Book 1: Fallen Ink

Book 2: Restless Ink

Book 2.5: Ashes to Ink

Book 3: Jagged Ink

Book 3.5: Ink by Numbers

Montgomery Ink Denver:

Book 0.5: Ink Inspired

Book 0.6: Ink Reunited

Book 1: Delicate Ink

Book 1.5: Forever Ink

Book 2: Tempting Boundaries

Book 3: Harder than Words

Book 3.5: Finally Found You

Book 4: Written in Ink

Book 4.5: Hidden Ink

Book 5: Ink Enduring

Book 6: Ink Exposed

Book 6.5: Adoring Ink

Book 6.6: Love, Honor, & Ink

Book 7: Inked Expressions

Book 7.3: Dropout

Book 7.5: Executive Ink

Book 8: Inked Memories

Book 8.5: Inked Nights

Book 8.7: Second Chance Ink

Book 8.5: Montgomery Midnight Kisses

Bonus: Inked Kingdom

The On My Own Series:

Book 0.5: My First Glance

Book 1: My One Night

Book 2: My Rebound

Book 3: My Next Play

Book 4: My Bad Decisions

The Promise Me Series:

Book 1: Forever Only Once

Book 2: From That Moment

Book 3: Far From Destined

Book 4: From Our First

The Less Than Series:

Book 1: Breathless With Her

Book 2: Reckless With You

Book 3: Shameless With Him

The Fractured Connections Series:

Book 1: Breaking Without You

Book 2: Shouldn't Have You

Book 3: Falling With You

Book 4: Taken With You

The Whiskey and Lies Series:

Book 1: <u>Whiskey Secrets</u>

Book 2: <u>Whiskey Reveals</u>

Book 3: <u>Whiskey Undone</u>

The Gallagher Brothers Series:

Book 1: <u>Love Restored</u>

Book 2: <u>Passion Restored</u>

Book 3: <u>Hope Restored</u>

The Ravenwood Coven Series:

Book 1: Dawn Unearthed

Book 2: Dusk Unveiled

Book 3: Evernight Unleashed

The Talon Pack:

Book 1: <u>Tattered Loyalties</u>

Book 2: <u>An Alpha's Choice</u>

Book 3: <u>Mated in Mist</u>

Book 4: <u>Wolf Betrayed</u>

Book 5: <u>Fractured Silence</u>

Book 6: <u>Destiny Disgraced</u>

Book 7: <u>Eternal Mourning</u>

Book 8: <u>Strength Enduring</u>

Book 9: <u>Forever Broken</u>

Book 10: Mated in Darkness

Book 11: Fated in Winter

Redwood Pack Series:

Book 1: <u>An Alpha's Path</u>

Book 2: <u>A Taste for a Mate</u>

Book 3: <u>Trinity Bound</u>

Book 3.5: <u>A Night Away</u>

Book 4: <u>Enforcer's Redemption</u>

Book 4.5: <u>Blurred Expectations</u>

Book 4.7: <u>Forgiveness</u>

Book 5: <u>Shattered Emotions</u>

Book 6: <u>Hidden Destiny</u>

Book 6.5: <u>A Beta's Haven</u>

Book 7: <u>Fighting Fate</u>

Book 7.5: <u>Loving the Omega</u>

Book 7.7: <u>The Hunted Heart</u>

Book 8: <u>Wicked Wolf</u>

The Elements of Five Series:

Book 1: From Breath and Ruin

Book 2: From Flame and Ash

Book 3: From Spirit and Binding

Book 4: From Shadow and Silence

Dante's Circle Series:

Book 1: <u>Dust of My Wings</u>

Book 2: <u>Her Warriors' Three Wishes</u>

Book 3: <u>An Unlucky Moon</u>

Book 3.5: <u>His Choice</u>

Book 4: <u>Tangled Innocence</u>

Book 5: <u>Fierce Enchantment</u>

Book 6: <u>An Immortal's Song</u>

Book 7: <u>Prowled Darkness</u>

Book 8: Dante's Circle Reborn

Holiday, Montana Series:

Book 1: <u>Charmed Spirits</u>

Book 2: <u>Santa's Executive</u>

Book 3: <u>Finding Abigail</u>

Book 4: <u>Her Lucky Love</u>

Book 5: Dreams of Ivory

The Branded Pack Series:

    (Written with Alexandra Ivy)

    Book 1: <u>Stolen and Forgiven</u>

    Book 2: <u>Abandoned and Unseen</u>

    Book 3: <u>Buried and Shadowed</u>

A NOTE FROM CARRIE ANN RYAN

Thank you so much for reading **A Wilder Wedding!**

I had so much fun writing this romance and I truly have been waiting for them since book 1! Of course, their story was NOTHING like I planned and that's always the best ways haha. Wyatt's story is next in Forever For Us and yes...secrets are to be told. FINALLY!

If you'd like to read Eliza's story, you can find it in Inked Obsession!

The Wilder Brothers Series:

Book 1: One Way Back to Me

Book 2: Always the One for Me

Book 3: The Path to You

Book 4: Coming Home for Us

Book 5: Stay Here With Me

Book 6: Finding the Road to Us

Book 7: Moments for You

Book 7.5: A Wilder Wedding

Book 8: Forever For Us

Next in the Wilder Brothers Series:
Things get interesting with Wyatt and Ava:
Forever For Us

If you want to make sure you know what's coming next from me, you can sign up for my newsletter at www.CarrieAnnRyan.com; follow me on twitter at @CarrieAnnRyan, or like my Facebook page. I also have a Facebook Fan Club where we have trivia, chats, and other goodies. You guys are the reason I get to do what I do and I thank you.

Make sure you're signed up for my MAILING LIST so you can know when the next releases are available as well as find giveaways and FREE READS.

Happy Reading!

A NIGHT FOR US

Eli Wilder is at a loss. Due to tragedy, time, and life in general, he and his five brothers are suddenly getting out of the military at the same time.

Only none of them have any idea what to do next.

Eli might have a plan—one so far-fetched it will take a miracle for them to agree to it.

When he takes a chance, however, he meets the perfect woman. One he hadn't expected.

Now he has one night to prove he's the right man for the job—and for her.

CHAPTER TEN

Eli

Home is where the heart is. Or maybe just where you rest your boots after a long day. A long week. Hell, a long twenty years.

I wasn't even forty years old yet, and here I was, retired. Or at least as retired as one could be after putting in twenty with the military. I had put my entire life and career towards one goal, and now I was out. There was no going back. I was never going to work for the military again as a civilian or get a GS —general scale—position. I was just me...in this house I was renting because I wasn't sure where I wanted to live, but it was my home for now.

My boots were in the closet, scuffed and worn, and most likely headed towards the trash pile.

But I wore my new boots, ones that I was just now wearing in, getting to fit around my feet. And I had a roof over my head, and I suppose my heart was in it. Therefore, this was home.

I pinched the bridge of my nose and let out a breath. I clearly needed more coffee if I was going to pick apart a saying and add poetry of my own.

"Why did you ask us over here if you're just going to growl at yourself the whole time?" Evan asked from the doorway into the kitchen, and I turned to see my brother standing there, his posture rigid, slight lines of pain around his eyes. He was still getting used to the new prosthetic, but with therapy and a whole shit-ton of doctors, Evan was able to stand here in my kitchen on his own accord, with a glare on his face. Of course, the glare had always been there, even before the IED.

"Seriously though, are you going to come in with the rest of us? We got the barbecue."

"From Harmon's?" I asked, my stomach rumbling.

"Of course we got it from Harmon's," Everett

called out from the living room, and I snorted before grabbing the six-pack of beer I had for this occasion.

I followed Evan out of the kitchen and into the living room, where Everett, Elijah, East, and Elliot were already lounging. We could have sat in a dining room, but I didn't have a large enough table for us. So we would be sprawling on my worn couch and used armchairs. I hadn't been able to get furniture of my own all my life. Or at least my adult life. I had moved from place to place, starting out in the barracks, and then I used rented furniture from the military because I was either overseas or living on base. When I had moved off base, I had put most of my money away and hadn't bothered with expensive furniture. Now I had furniture that I got from thrift stores and garage sales. Most guys I knew my age and rank had household items that didn't look like they belonged to a young bachelor. But all of them were married and had families. I'd run from mine.

"What is with this couch?" Elijah asked, sitting nearly ramrod straight at the edge of it. "We're adults now. Shouldn't you have something that isn't so brown and lumpy that you can sink into?"

Evan grunted as he sat into the armchair, resting

his leg straight out in front of him. "This chair isn't that bad, but it's not good."

I flipped them both off as I handed everybody a beer and took a seat on the floor. I may be the eldest here, but my brothers had already claimed the chairs, so I was stuck with this. "Honestly, I was just thinking that I needed new shit, but first, I need a house. One that's not a rental."

"It's still a good time for the market," Elliot put in, looking down at his phone. He bounced his foot quickly as he spoke, and I held back a snort at that.

"I know it's a good time in the market." That was a decent segue, so I let out a breath. "However, I don't want to buy a house."

East's eyes widened. "What do you want to buy?"

I looked at my brothers, at the five of them that were my best friends. Between them and our youngest sister Eliza, there were seven of us. All named with an E, and all different in the same way. Somehow all six of us brothers had joined the Air Force and had rarely lived in the same place. It was hard enough to find a position that worked for you in the military for long, let alone finding a place that was near one of your siblings. It just didn't work out that way. I had been on tour at the same time with at least one sibling, but we were never stationed in the same place. They did that on purpose, from back in the days when wars would take out entire squadrons, and therefore an entire set of siblings. But I still felt like it had been years since I'd really gotten to know my brothers. Now we were all in the same place, *retired*.

Evan didn't want to be here, but I knew it wasn't because of family. No, he had his own reasons for not wanting to move back to San Antonio. We had lived here before when we had been kids, the seven of us, and it felt like home when we'd been little. We could have moved out west to where our uncles had lived on the winery, but that hadn't felt right. Now we were here in Texas trying to make our own home.

San Antonio had enough bases, so many military people retired in the area. It was gorgeous, decent weather if you liked the heat, and it was within driving distance of hill country, wine country, desert, city, and even the beach if you wanted to drive around five hours. It was a good area, and I was glad that this was where we were putting down our roots.

Although, Eliza wasn't moving down with us. When the guys and I had all planned where we were going to retire, I had always assumed Eliza would come with us. And then she had lost her husband in an IED explosion, the catalyst for why all of us Wilders had gotten out when we had.

Between Evan's accident, and Eliza's husband's, we hadn't wanted to stay in anymore. I had reached my twenty while the others hadn't, but we were all out. Though Eliza had found love again somehow and was up in Fort Collins with her husband's family. I didn't begrudge her for that, and I knew we would all be visiting our little sister often, but it was still odd that she wasn't going to be with us.

Either way, though, we were here—the Wilder brothers. Evan was growly and not exactly pleasant at the moment. It had nothing to do with his pain, though, and all to do with his past.

Everett liked it here, at least from what I could tell. He was the quietest of us all, and sometimes it was hard for me to figure out exactly what he was thinking at all times.

Elijah was out of his depth and angry but always had a smile on his face. He was also the only one that actually liked wearing a suit, so maybe he would like what I had in store for us. I wasn't sure, though.

East knew what he wanted, though he never told us. He was growly, a little abrasive, but considering what he used to do, it worked for him. But I knew he needed roots, needed to settle with us, and so that's why we were here. To keep him safe. To keep all of us safe. Including Elliot, the youngest of the brothers, though still older than Eliza by a couple of years. He had gone out earlier than all of us for his own reasons. And I knew of all of them. He was going to click with what I had in mind more than the rest. At least, that's what I hoped.

"Seriously? Why are we here?" Evan growled and then let out a sigh.

I figured I might as well tell them what my plans were, even if they felt insane. "I don't plan on living in this house for long. It's a rental, and I do want to buy. Just not a house."

"You said that, but what do you mean?" Everett asked as he leaned forward over our meal.

"I want to buy land."

They blinked up at me, and Evan tilted his head. "You want to be a rancher? Or just buy land with a lot of oaks?"

I snorted, thinking of the land for sale around us. The market was hot and many people moving out here wanted the land for privacy, not necessarily for what it had been used for in the past. "The place I'm looking at has a few oaks, but not a ranch. No, I want to buy land that is far more expensive than what I can afford alone."

They all looked at me then, while Elijah leaned forward. His normal smile tilted down, and he frowned. "You mean the inheritance? From our uncles?"

Our mother's brothers had both passed within the last year, and we were the only family that they had. When they died, their winery had been sold, as required by the will, but the proceeds from it, as well as whatever holdings they had, went to *us*. Meaning we had a decent nest egg on its way, and none of us had been expecting it or planning on it. So I had plans of my own. I just had to hope that they agreed.

"There's a piece of land that I want to buy. And I want to make it a retreat. Or, rather, continue the property as a retreat with our own touches."

"What the hell are you talking about?" Evan snarled.

"Yeah, you want to spend money that we don't have yet? I mean, I know it was out of the blue, but what the fuck?" East put in.

I held up my hand. "We all need something to do. Right now, we're working in dead-end jobs to give us an income and to pay our bills, but none of us were expecting to get out when we did." I looked at all of them, and they swallowed hard, nodding.

"It's hard to find a new career when you thought you already had one," Elijah whispered. Elijah had been a meteorologist for the Air Force, but the degree he had finally been able to get wasn't in meteorology. It was hard to find a job in the field that he was trained in when he didn't have the right degree for a civilian. But he was brilliant in more than that, and I hoped he realized that.

"Just let me finish," I began. "I want to open up a retreat. A Wilder Retreat. And the land that I'm looking at, the land I've already spoken to the owners about, is a place where we can make it an inn. Host weddings, and there's even a winery attached. The owners are fine with wanting to change the name of the company, too. I wouldn't have done it if they'd had a strong connection to it. We can make Wilder fucking Wines." They all looked at me like I was insane, and maybe I was. But I had plans. "Before you think I've lost my mind, I've been talking to Roy."

"Roy, wait, didn't he open up a place like it outside of Austin?" Everett asked, frowning.

"He did. That's where I got the idea. We all need something to do, and we've all been living on our own and away from each other for long enough that it feels like we're not even the same brothers anymore." They were all silent so I kept going. "I want us to work together. I want us to start a business."

"The Wilder Retreat," Evan growled. "What's our tagline? Let loose and get wild?"

I ran my hand through my hair, knowing our dinner was getting cold, but I had started about this the wrong way. "Fuck I don't know. But we plan things. We can do this."

Everett moved forward. "We're military. We trained in explosives and planes. We don't do wineries or fucking weddings or winery tours."

They were all saying things I had gone over in my head countless times, but the thing was, we were more than our past, and I had to hope to hell we figured that out. "I know that. But we can learn. The place that I'm looking at, the owner is an older man who wants to sell, and there's already staff in place that know what they're doing. We can fit in, find our way. We are more than just the jobs that we were given and trained for all our lives. We can do this. And we need a normal."

"And this would be a normal?" Elliot asked, but I saw the interest in his eyes.

"What do you want us to do for the rest of our lives? Work a desk job? Work for someone else? We've been working for someone else our entire lives. Let's work for ourselves. Let's make it our business."

"What would we do?" Evan asked, his voice low.

"We'll split the business. Each of us would have our own concept of what we're doing. We've all been in charge of organizing and setting up plans and strategizing. Our jobs as teens were like this, even if it's been a few years for some of us. Now, instead of the way that we operated in the military, we'll put it to use for running an inn and a winery."

"I like the taste of wine. I don't actually know how to make wine," Evan whispered.

I shook my head. "Of all of us, you know the most about wine. You worked with the uncles over our summers as a teen and even again every time you visited on whatever vacations you could take over the years."

Evan scowled. "Yeah, so I know a little bit, but I don't know enough to begin a new wine. I only know about the grapes from their place, not these."

"We are near Fredericksburg. They make great wines," Everett said, his eyes narrowing. Everett was brilliant. If he hadn't gone into the service, I knew he would have been an accountant or his own CEO or CFO. I knew he'd be the one to make sure that we didn't go bankrupt. He just didn't know it.

"Evan, they have a vintner, a winemaker. But they need someone to help as the Director. What Uncle Leo used to do and what you trained for before you joined up." Evan scowled at me, but it didn't look as menacing at least.

"So, what, we each get our own position and we figure out how to work together?" East asked, growling. "I'm good with my hands. I can build things. I don't want to work in hospitality or with fucking grapes."

I nodded tightly. "I know that East. So that could be your job. Things break down, and we need to build things. I have all this written out, and I was going to talk it over with you. But first, I want to make sure that's something that's feasible. On top of that, Roy invited us to a wedding."

"We're not fucking wedding planners," Evan growled.

I held up my hand. "That's why we would hire a wedding planner for that part. As for an event planner? I think we all know who among us could be that person. We could be the people that show off our area. To plan tours for the winery, or even downtown San Antonio, or anything for when somebody wants to relax. We have spent our whole lives working for the government, risking our lives. Now, let's enjoy it. Enjoy a home that we can build. And help others relax, too. I know it's insane. But I didn't want us to work together in a bar or build a company from the ground up. This place is already settled, and it has potential. We can hire someone for the wedding part, someone good. But we can do the rest."

"And Roy wants you to visit him then?" Elijah asked, speaking of my friend who had gotten out a couple of years before me, and had sparked this idea.

"He has a very similar concept a couple of hours from us. I want to see how it works, and you should come with us."

"So, we're going to crash a wedding?" Everett asked.

"Well, I was thinking you and I could. And at least take some notes. Everyone else has to work, and I figured some of you guys might not be in the mood for a wedding."

Evan grunted, and we all knew who I was talking about at that moment.

"This is insane," Elijah began, but held up his hand when I started to interrupt. "But I could see it.

We've all talked about getting out and working together. We just happened to get out far sooner than we planned."

There was silence in that, but we were good about not talking about the whys of it.

"So we're going to start over, work for ourselves, and we have the money to do this?" Everett asked as he pulled out his phone and started running numbers.

"We do. I hope. I'll send you what I have. The owner doesn't have any kids and wants to sell. He also wants to keep the business that he already has in place operating. He's one of us. Retired Air Force."

That made Evan's lips twitch. "I guess we can listen to him then."

I knew that would get Evan. We were a brotherhood, even those not by blood. I didn't know if this was going to work or if it was just a lark.

I wanted us to be together. I wanted us to work towards a common purpose. And if that meant going out on a limb and trying something completely crazy and something that could risk everything, then I would do it. We had risked our lives for longer than I cared to admit. Why not risk something else to find a home?

In order to be settled.

Everett and I could see Roy and realize that this wasn't what we wanted, and we'd find something else. This had shown up out of the blue, and it just spoke to me.

I was probably losing my goddam mind, but I didn't have anything else.

I wanted my brothers settled, and I was the eldest. I needed to make sure that they were safe and had a future. None of us were married, other than Eliza. None of us had a family. We had spent so long protecting others. Now it was time to think for ourselves.

So we would. And I would make sure that they had a path—that they had a future.

First, however, it was time to go to a wedding.

CHAPTER ELEVEN

Alexis

My job was to plan. And yet, I didn't think I could prepare for this.

"I just really wanted the sun to shine from the goddess on my wedding. And yet it feels as if she's crying." The bride paced in front of me, her hair in hot rollers, her eyes puffy from sobbing. I risked a look behind her at the bright sun and the single white puffy cloud in the sky. The cloud that was apparently sending this woman over the edge.

"It will be okay. The weather is still on our side."

I knocked on wood as I said it, knowing that's what she wanted me to do. And frankly, I would have done it anyway.

"Do you see that cloud? That cloud is mocking me on this day. It is mocking everything that I have stood for. Now how will I know if my love is true, knowing this cloud exists? I was supposed to be wed. To blend my soul with that of my mate and to know that our forever was only a beginning. And yet, it is over. Everything is over." She flung herself on the chaise lounge while her mother glared at me before patting her daughter's arm.

"We'll find a way to make this work. I know it's going to be hard, but don't you worry. We will find a way."

The bride began to sob in earnest. "Today was supposed to be about love and prosperity. I saw it happen."

I nodded even though she couldn't see me and knelt by her, putting on my best wedding planner tone. "Of course, it's about love and prosperity. You are going to marry the love of your life this afternoon."

"Will I? Or will that cloud ruin my destiny? For I was told that today was the day that we were supposed to be married. I saw it in the cards, as did my psychic. Don't you see? She told me today was the day."

I sat back on my heels and nodded sagely at her words, trying not to roll my eyes. I was of the mind that people were allowed to believe in whatever they wanted to, that there was more than one possibility for the world we were in.

And yet, right then, it was all a little too much for me. Mostly because everything had been planned by me, and therefore the psychic. The psychic had chosen this day for the wedding, so I had agreed to it. The psychic had read what color the wedding needed to be in tea leaves, so I had gone with it. My job was to make sure the bride was happy, and the groom as well, but mostly the bride in this case.

The groom just seemed happy that his bride had said yes after years of trying to get her to commit, and therefore I was here. To work on the Baylor Ranch and Brewery and to plan this wedding.

I truly loved this venue. Roy Baylor, the owner and operator of the retreat and venue was a wonderful man, a little strict, but knew what he wanted. And that meant making sure that the bride was happy.

Even if a single cloud in the sky was about to ruin her day, apparently.

"Okay now, let's think about what this cloud can signify," I began as my assistant walked in, her eyes wide at the scene in front of her. I waved her off, and Emily slowly backed out of the room, trying not to make a noise so she wouldn't get caught.

At least she was allowed to leave. Maybe she would be able to work with the caterer, the venue, and to ensure everything else was on track for the wedding that was supposed to begin in forty-five minutes.

I smiled softly and did what I did best: made the bride happy. "That single cloud can be evidence of the path you were once on. The path of you as a woman. But it is showing you that you are ready for the next phase. To the blue skies that will be your marriage." Emily gave me a thumbs-up as she walked out, and I did think that I had done pretty well just then in terms of making crap up.

"Do you think? Do you think that Reggie will be okay with this? That he won't leave me because of this cloud and what it can signify?"

I leaned down in front of Phoenix and held her hand. "You are a beautiful bride. Exquisite. You are marrying the love of your life. I cannot wait to see you in that dress and to watch the reaction of the love of your life as he sees you for the first time today."

She patted her lip, her pout slowly decreasing. "It is a beautiful dress."

"And you are the beautiful woman in that dress. He is going to marry you, not because of the signs, but because he loves you. And that cloud is not the shadow upon your day. It is just a mere moment in time, signifying it is the next phase of your life. It is time for you to marry your Reggie. For Reggie and Phoenix to have a wedding on the books like no other."

I wasn't lying then. This would be a wedding like no other.

"Do you think?" she asked as her mother continued to wipe tears from her face.

"I do. Now let's get you finished with your hair and makeup. And then in that dress. Reggie's waiting. Much like that cloud was waiting for you to see it so it could depart, and you can know that your day is in perfect harmony."

One of the bridesmaids rolled her eyes, and I gently narrowed mine, warning her not to say anything. She grinned wide, and I ignored her and went to help the bride finish getting ready. Knowing she was in good hands with the rest of the wedding party, I went to my other duties, focusing on the caterer and whatever else came up.

The best man walked past, his face a little too bright, and I leaned forward and handed him a mint and a bottle of water from the side table. "Eat this and drink this. No more pregaming before the wedding."

He smiled at me, a little sloppily. "Yeah, I know. I'm just trying to walk it off."

That was good to hear, at least. "No worries, we will make sure that this wedding is amazing. Just stay a little more hydrated."

"You've got it, boss. Thanks, Ms. Alexis."

I waved him off. "It's what I'm here for."

The venue had its own florist and caterer, so I didn't have to use my contacts, which was nice. Not all venues had that, nor did they have their own planning stations. I liked working with places like that felt as if they were resorts. Those didn't tend to have an on-hand wedding planner, but an event planner where I could step in and do my part of the job. Sometimes it got a little hard to mix the two, but Jeff and I worked well together. Right now, he was working on another event for the company while I was working on this wedding. Some guests at the resort weren't part of the wedding itself, and so it was Jeff's job to make sure that they had something to do that would not interfere with the wedding. Now mine was all about the ceremony and following reception. I checked over the cake one more time and made sure everybody was in their place.

"Blue alert, blue alert," Emily said into my headset, and I held back a sigh.

"Blue?" I asked as I made my way to her.

"It's not quite urgent, but it does have to do with the color of the bridesmaids' dresses," Emily whispered fiercely as I came to her side.

"What is it?" I asked, and then I didn't need her to explain.

One of the bridesmaids, Jasmine, if I remembered correctly, was not wearing the correct dress. Oh, it was the right color, but it used to have far more fabric than it currently did.

"Crap on a cracker," I mumbled.

Emily blinked. "Is that the saying?"

"It is now. Okay, let me handle this." I rolled my shoulders back and smiled as Emily went to deal with another part of our checklist. I looked at Jasmine as the other woman just narrowed her gaze, put her hand on her hip, and showed off a generous amount of leg.

"You can't tell me what to do," Jasmine snapped, and from there, I knew that the other woman had planned this on purpose because she wanted to be the showcase of the day.

Well, screw that. This was what I was good at and what I was going to fix.

"You look wonderful, Jasmine. Though the dress is a little bit different than what we had planned on, correct?"

"Oh, I had always planned on this. Phoenix has always been a little too much. You know? This will put her down a peg."

I smiled through my teeth, even as my eyes went cold. Jasmine must have seen the look because her hand fell, and she raised her chin defiantly. "Today is about Phoenix. And Reggie. And their love for one another. While you do look amazing, this is not the dress you agreed on."

"There's no way you can add more to it. I've already had it altered."

I nodded tightly. "Oh, I know. However, when there's a will, there's a way."

I looked to the side as Emily came running

forward, our seamstress right beside her. "Now come on, I know exactly what you need to do."

"There's not enough time," Jasmine snapped.

"Arabella is brilliant at what she does. We'll make the time."

Arabella's eyebrows winged to the top of her forehead as she took in the gown. "It's a good thing I've brought extra fabric. You never know when you're going to need to add an entire skirt."

The defiance on Jasmine's gaze didn't alter. "You will not be touching me or my dress."

I raised a brow. "And if you continue to think that way, you will not be in the wedding."

"This is not your day. You don't get to tell me what to do." Her lower lip wobbled and while I wondered what might have happened between the two women in the past to lead them here, my job was to ensure the bride was happy without hurting anyone in the process. Finding that balance was a tap dance.

Thankfully I'd taken lessons.

"No, this is Phoenix's day. And actually, I do get to tell you what to do. This is not the same dress that the others had decided on, therefore, you will have to wear something appropriate for Phoenix. I'm not going to tell you what's appropriate in general or in life, just what the bride wants. And today is about what the bride wants."

"She's just going to get divorced in a minute anyway. She and Reggie aren't even good for each other. He liked me first."

This wasn't something I was going to get into. I didn't have it in me. Nor did I care. I turned toward the seamstress and gave her a genuine smile. "Thank you, Arabella."

Arabella grinned. "Don't you worry. I'll get it taken care of."

"You're not listening to me," Jasmine snapped, and I tilted my head and smiled at her, knowing it didn't quite reach my eyes.

"Today is not about you. Or me. This is about the bride and the groom. This is their moment. You don't get to ruin it. Even if you might feel differently. When it is over, you can have a lovely talk with Phoenix, and I will understand. But for now, you will fix your dress, you will walk down the aisle and smile, and you will be the beautiful woman that I know you are, inside and out." That was stretching it a bit, but with the way that Jasmine's eyes warmed slightly, I had to hope that that was the right trick. "You can do this, Jasmine. You can show the world that you can handle anything."

"He was mine," Jasmine murmured.

My heart hurt for her, even though I was slightly cold inside when it came to love these days. Not that I was going to mention that. "But he's hers now. And you said yes to the wedding. Be a good friend. Show that you love them both."

"Fine," Jasmine snapped and turned to follow Arabella.

"That was one disaster levied," Emily whispered just by my side, and I nodded tightly.

"We'll keep an eye on her."

"I'll do that since you have the other thousand things to do."

I shook my head. "We'll do it together. We have twenty minutes until go time. Time to go through our checklist one more time."

We nodded at each other then went to work, fixing the maid of honor's shoe and then the flower crown for the flower girl. The ring bearer currently had his finger halfway up his nose, so I helped wash his hands and anchored him to one of the groomsmen who could handle the kid. I walked from pew to pew, ensuring that each flower arrangement was where it needed to be, and as the minister nodded at me, a gentle smile on his face, I knew we were almost there.

So close.

Roy stopped me on my way to the bride and grinned. "Good job, Alexis."

I smiled at the older man and shook my head. "Not yet. Almost there, though."

"Of course, can't put the cart before the horse and all that."

"You sound more and more Texan every day." I winked.

He let out a rough chuckle. "I try. Now, I'll see you after the wedding. Save me a dance."

I rolled my eyes, knowing Roy was happily married but was doing his best to try to get me out on the dance floor because apparently I needed to have a life. I had a life, thank you very much. It just didn't have anything to do with weddings. Other than the fact that my entire life was weddings. Just not my own.

Once the wedding began, I had my eyes on every person that I could at the same time, narrowing them at Jasmine as she walked in her now full gown, Arabella's magic to die for. Jasmine looked like a princess herself, a little manic, but didn't ruin the wedding. And when Phoenix walked down the aisle underneath the blue skies—without a single cloud —I smiled and let out a relieved breath.

The first part was now over, now for the actual reception where things were just getting started.

My photographer was set up for photos, and I let Emily handle half of them when I ensured that the rest of the wedding guests were doing their thing in the reception. They were going for a buffet, so people could mingle and party about, and the dance floor would be rocking soon. First, though, we had a few other things to handle, and I was exhausted. I should probably sleep a little bit more before big weddings, but I had too much on my plate.

When the bride and the groom made their entrance, I smiled, and Emily wiped away a tear.

"They're just so beautiful."

"They are," I agreed. I also didn't think they would last long, but maybe they would surprise me. I liked when they surprised me. I wanted love to last, even though sometimes it didn't, and it broke you.

Emily nudged me, and I looked over at her, shaking my head. "What? Is something wrong?"

"Look over at *them*. All tall, dark, and handsome. And growly. I want to take a bite of that. Who are they?"

I laughed. I couldn't help it. One of the guests gave me a look and smiled, and I held back a wince.

My job was to blend into the scenes, not to make noise and laugh. I had to be better than that.

I stared over at the two men with dark hair and blue eyes and frowned. I didn't recognize them, and I had to wonder what side of the wedding they were from. I frowned, going through my mental list, but figured they had to be someone on the groom's side since I didn't know everybody by their face. However, they seemed to be brothers and were attractive, though I didn't swoon like Emily seemed to be doing. Barely.

"Seriously though, who are they? And are they single?"

"You can find out after the wedding. We do not mix pleasure with business. You know that."

Emily put her hand over her heart and mimicked it beating while she fluttered her eyelashes at me. "Don't you wish we did, though?" she purred, and I shook my head before I met the gaze of the slightly older man. His blue eyes intensified and narrowed on mine before a shiver went down my spine. I swallowed hard, and broke the connection, and looked down at Emily.

"Not for us. You know that."

"Spoilsport. But I suppose we have to get back to work."

I swallowed hard and then looked back to where the man had been standing, only to find the space empty, and sighed. "Time to work. It's what we're good at."

And I pushed the thoughts of the man with the blue eyes from my mind, knowing I had far more important things to worry about tonight.

CHAPTER TWELVE

Eli

"Why did I say I'd wear a tie?" Everett asked as he worked his collar.

I snorted and looked over at my younger brother. "Because it's a wedding and its formal, and we were told by Roy we *had* to wear a tie. It's not my fault you borrowed Elijah's rather than buying one for yourself."

Everett sighed, worked his collar again. "I know I'm going to need to buy an actual suit that fits if we do this. It's also not my fault that I looked damn fine in my dress blues, but my shoulders outgrew my old suit. Hell, I'm going to be the CFO, damn it, I should look the part."

I held back a grin, knowing that Everett might be growling slightly at the plan, but I knew he was in. Of all of my brothers, he was the most into it. That was Everett. Quiet sometimes, but determined.

"You're in then? CFO and everything? You've got the background and the degree for it."

Everett gave me a look, a single brow raised. "Of course, I'm in. I was in when you first mentioned it, even though it sounds insane."

I held back a laugh since I didn't want to draw too much attention to us. "I guess that would make me CEO. Though I don't want to think about being your boss."

Everett shook his head. "You've always been our boss. You're the big brother. The only one you couldn't order around is Eliza, but then again, none of us can order around our little sister."

That made my lips twitch, and I took a sip of the champagne the waiter had brought about. I wasn't a huge champagne fan, but it tasted good, and I felt like I needed the liquid courage to be here. It was odd to be somewhat crashing a wedding, though Roy said we could come as observers. We weren't going to eat or draw attention to ourselves, but it was good to watch what Roy and his team were doing. I knew there was a wedding planner around somewhere, one that Roy hired on since he didn't have one on staff. However, Roy was thinking about hiring someone permanently.

If the Wilders did go along with this insane plan, we'd be following Roy's footsteps to the letter.

"I don't know how to take that. Am I bossy?"

Everett grinned. "Yes. You're colossally bossy. It's what you do. Then again, you were the only officer among us."

I shrugged. "I got lucky with a scholarship and placement right out of high school, and things worked out for me. I was also in longer than any of you."

"And now we're all out, a bunch of NCOs without jobs."

"Local accounting jobs at the warehouses not doing it for you?" I teased.

"I hope that this works out because I'd rather you be my boss than anyone else. Yeah, you get annoying sometimes, but you're my brother. I wiped your brow after you threw up after too many drinks. I feel like that connects us."

I snorted. I couldn't help it. "You did that for

East. He's your twin. Not for me. I'm a little too old for that."

There was a seven-year age gap between the twins and me, even more so between Elliott and me and Eliza. There were seven of us, and honestly, not too many years between us. I didn't know how my parents had done it, and never got a chance to ask before they died.

"Think we can do this?" I asked after a moment, looking at the party in front of us.

"Plan a wedding? No. Do everything else? Yes, I think we can."

I looked at him then, my eyes wide. "Just like that."

"Not just like that. You had notebooks and files on what it takes. And we're going to that workshop about inns and owning your own business."

"One where Roy promises it's not a timeshare scam." We both laughed at that before I continued. "We'll learn, and we've got the money to do it. I mean, I guess we could use the money for other things, but this is for our future, not just for a new car or new house."

Everett's lips twitch. "Considering most of us will end up living on the property if things work out well, it *is* a new house. And we've got decent cars.

And there'll be enough after we buy the place to hopefully to get a new truck or two since we'll need it. For hauling."

"And because we live in Texas and need to fit in," I said with a laugh.

"And you know that Evan is going to thrive on the winery side."

I swallowed hard at Everett's words. "He will. If he lets himself."

"That's a big if. But, hell, he's the one who worked with the uncles for the longest. He's the main reason that we even had this opportunity. Not that we can let him know that."

I smiled despite myself. "You're right. We could figure things out but he's the glue. We each have a job. Each have a purpose. We work together. We wouldn't split up, take too much time away from each other like we've been doing for twenty years. Hell, I left the house to go pursue my own future when you guys were babies."

"I wasn't a baby. Sure, Eliza was, but I wasn't."

My lips twitched. "Close enough since you were like in puberty."

Everett sighed, looked over his shoulder. "Please, say that loudly for the people on the other side of the ball ballroom."

I looked around the vast room with the elevated ceilings and twinkling lights. "Our ballroom won't look like this."

"True, but ours would be in a renovated European-style farmhouse. The place is in good shape. It's like a fucking villa."

I snorted at the look of one of the guests at our cursing. "That was the goal for the original builders. They wanted to bring a little bit of Europe here with the architecture. So it is a villa of sorts in the middle of south Texas."

"Well, this is a little more upper-class farm."

I nodded. "We won't be competing for each other, even though we're a couple of hours away."

"Which is a good thing because we like Roy and need his help. We don't want to piss him off."

"Why don't you want to piss me off?" Roy asked as he walked over to us. Roy was a big man, mostly still muscle after all these years as a civilian, and he took care of himself. His hair was graying at the temples, and his full beard was white and gray now. He looked good, and he had been my friend for years. We had fought together, had been neighbors and even roommates for a bit in our early years. He was a couple of years older than me, so he got out before I did, but we had stayed in touch and, hopefully, he'd be able to help me figure out exactly what the hell I was going to do with the rest of my life.

"We were just thinking about taking your business," Everett said with a grin, and Roy just threw his head back and laughed, that big deep laugh that made everyone around us smile. Nobody glared at him. He was just the good guy who people got along with wherever he went.

Maybe that's why he was so good at this. I wasn't that guy. Whatever it was. Everett was. As was Elijah. And Elliot. East, Evan, and I were a little more on the asshole side of the family. But half of us being assholes, the other half being decent guys wasn't a bad mark.

"You're welcome to try, though. I think with the winery on your side and the brewery on mine, it's a good fit. We'll be able to send whoever can't fit into ours to each other. Working like a partnership, rather than adversaries."

The way that Roy said it, it seemed like a decree, and frankly, I agreed. "Sounds good to me. And honestly, it'll be nice having footsteps to follow in, even if we're trying to be our own bosses."

"I had footsteps too. The guy who owned this before I was a retired general."

"No shit?" I asked.

"Two star. Wanted something with his life a little bit different, and this was in the family. He sold it to me, and now you're buying from a former military man as well. It's all in the family, even though our family's a bit convoluted."

"Don't even begin on the whole convoluted family thing," Everett added with a grin.

Roy let out a big belly laugh that drew a few gazes our way. "There are seven of you, all starting with the same letter. What the hell was your mother thinking?"

I just smiled, used to the refrain. It had been worse when we'd all been active duty and went by Wilder. "We answered to numbers mostly. I was one."

"I don't remember my number. I think mom forgot it too." Everett said with a grin.

Roy leaned forward, laughing. "Well, you're a twin. I'm sure you and East switched off often just to annoy your parents."

"I can neither confirm nor deny."

Roy just grinned. "Well, you've had a look around. You saw the books and figured out what we do. What is it that you want?"

Everett looked to me, and I swallowed hard, rolling my shoulders back. "We want something that we can work together in. The place that we're looking at we would rename to Wilder Resorts. It has a good flow. It just needs some updating, but we can do that. Especially within the budget. We're already in talks, and they're not talking with anybody else right now for selling, so that's a good thing."

"Time is still on your side," Roy added.

"For sure. There are twenty cabins outside of the main building. The main building is a villa, with its own atrium and dining room and breakfast room and all that. The innkeeper can live there. And then within the cabins, we can designate some of those for the family like they did, so we can live on the property and not have to pay rent or mortgages on other places."

"That makes sense. We live in a house on the property. If you live in those cabins, are you going to cut into your bottom line?"

I shook my head. "No, this is what the other owners did before us with their teams. It makes sense. And while we all did training for other things when we were active duty, all of our degrees went towards what we thought we'd do as civilians versus what we did in the service. Oh, and we can take the cabins that need the most work for ourselves and work on them on our own."

Everett snorted. "Thanks for giving us the heaps to live in."

I raised a brow. "You've seen our land. There's nothing heap about it."

"That is true," Everett whispered.

"There's a pool, a sunning area with a shit-ton of tile that's perfect for photos according to the owner's daughter. And then, on the other side of the acreage, there's a winery with forested trails. There's a tasting room, barrel rooms, a large building for all the equipment. It's like its own business on the property."

Roy nodded along as we went over everything again. "And it's a lot of acres, more than I have. But then again, you need more land for the vines. Not that it's a huge heap of vines, but a respectable amount for good wines in moderation."

"It's a shit ton, but pricing right now is good, and I think we can make it work."

"I'm here if you need me, but it's a good opportunity. Yeah, it's different than what any of you guys did in the military, but hell, most of us were just handed an instruction packet once we joined, after we took a test to see what we were most suited for.

Not that we knew what we were suited for, and then we went into that field. You can do that here."

I nodded. "We can. And hell, this might be nice. Something completely different."

"You're jumping into hospitality, think you can do it?"

I sighed, looked at my brother. "I think I want to."

"I don't think, I know." Everett grinned and then reached out and squeezed my other shoulder.

"Now to convince the others." That made me wince but Everett looked unfazed.

"They're not going to need convincing," Everett said with a tight nod. "They're already excited. Or at least as excited as they can be with their scowls."

"I sure do love your family," Roy said with a laugh. "And look, the garter toss is about to begin, go boys, go see if you're the next to get wed."

I blinked, looked at Roy. "I thought you said we needed to be casual observers."

"True, but there aren't as many single men here as there are single women, so go stand over there and fill the place so that way it's not three guys vying for a garter."

"Isn't that kind of archaic?" Everett asked, and I snorted.

"What he said. I'm not going to go catch a fucking garter."

"Go. Stand there. Don't hold out your hands. Just stand there and look forward. Fill up the space."

"I don't understand you," I grumbled.

"You don't have to. You just have to do what I say."

"He did outrank you," Everett said with a grin, and I flipped my brother off before I lowered my head at Roy's glare, and walked over to where the dozen or so men were standing, hands in pockets, looking for all the world they would rather be anywhere else.

"They needed men for this, my ass," I grumbled, and Everett snorted.

"Hey, look on the bright side, the odds work in our favor now that we won't catch it, which is good. We have enough on our plate without getting married."

"My mom forced me over here, so I'm going to hide behind you," a man in his early twenties said as he smiled over at us. "If that's okay."

"Fuck no, you're not hiding behind me. I don't want the damn thing," I growled.

Everett just grinned, the asshole. "Nobody does,

but here we are, at a place where love and happy ever after is the only thing that matters."

I shook my head and stood there, hands in pockets as the bride sat down on a chair, and everybody started to cheer. Music began, and the groom went down on his knees, slid his hands up the bride's dress, and slowly, very slowly took her garter down.

"Well then, I feel like we're part of a peep show," Everett mumbled out of the side of his mouth, and I elbowed him to keep him quiet. He let out an oof, and when the groom stood up, swung the garter over his head, I held back a sigh. Apparently, we would have to get used to this, because a big part of the income were events and weddings on the property. I was going to have to start enjoying shit like this if this is what I wanted to do with the rest of my life.

Everybody started shouting, laughing, and I looked up as the garter was flung from the groom's hand and slapped me directly in the chest. On instinct, I reached out and gripped it and blinked.

"Fuck," Everett said with a laugh as everybody cheered.

"Better you than me," the younger man said before he rushed off to where his mom stood. The kid's mom glared at me, and I looked down at the frilly white thing and just shook my head.

"Well, shit," I grumbled.

"Oh, look at you, you're the next to be wed. I'm so proud," Everett teased as he wiped away a fake tear.

Everybody started congratulating me, and there were a few curious looks, probably wondering where the hell I had come from. I was supposed to be lowkey for this wedding, and here I was catching the fucking garter.

We moved out of the way as the bride came back, tossing bouquet in hand. "Okay single ladies, let's see who's going to get a ring on it!"

I held back a groan at the cheesy joke and watched as a few dozen women all lined up, jokingly ready to fight for the bouquet.

My gaze caught the eyes of one woman as she stood off to the side, earbud in her ear as she looked around at the others. This had to be the wedding planner, the woman that I had seen before and nearly swallowed my tongue over.

"You're drooling," Everett whispered.

"She's hot. Can't help it."

"And she's not for you. Remember? We said no dating."

"When did we say that?" I asked as I shook my head.

"You're gone, just like that, one look, and you're gone."

I didn't answer. Instead, I watched as the bride tossed the bouquet, but she sort of twisted her body as she did so, laughing and probably a little bit drunk. The bouquet flew over the heads of the rest of the party and slammed into the wedding planner's face. She caught the bouquet, her eyes wide, and looked beyond mortified.

"Oh my God, I love it!" the bride screamed. "I knew the tea leaves said this. I knew it! Now, where's our garter man. We have to see the dance!"

I met the gaze of the wedding planner, and then I looked down at my garter and then back up again.

"Well shit."

CHAPTER THIRTEEN

Eli

I shouldn't have been surprised when Roy's hand pressed on my shoulder and practically pushed me towards the woman holding the bouquet.

"Dance! Dance! Dance!"

The crowd cheered, egging us on, and I found myself standing in front of the wedding planner, her soft blue suit nearly gray, and noticed that it was also a dress of some sort. She looked regal and yet like she wanted to blend with the background—something I should have been doing as well.

"This is not happening," she mumbled under her breath, and my eyes widened.

"Nice." I hadn't meant to say that aloud, but damn, I was the only one who was supposed to not want to be there. Not her.

She blushed and looked up at me. "Sorry."

The bride moved forward, her eyes bright and a bit manic. "Dance! Come on, Alexis. It's my wedding. And I want you to dance, darling."

The wedding planner leaned forward, and I tried not to inhale her rich scent. "Phoenix, I need to help with the next part of the setup."

"You can do that after you dance." The bride put her smile towards me, all teeth and manic eyes. "And, hello stranger. I don't know who you are, so you're probably with my lovely groom. However, you are about to dance with one of my bestest friends. This is my wedding planner. Wedding planner, this is the stranger."

"Eli. My name is Eli."

The bride gave me another shark-tooth smile. "Good. Eli, darling. Now, dance. Dance for me, my pretties!" she said with a clap of her hands as her groom came forward, rolled his eyes, and pulled her back.

The groom grinned. "Just do what she says, and

it'll all be over quick." He winked as he said it, then kissed his bride's neck, and she let out a little giggle. The two seemed in love, and like they were perfect for one another, even if the bride seemed a little high-strung. However, it was her wedding, so for all I knew, this was just an abnormality.

"Come on, let's just get this over with," the wedding planner mumbled under her breath as she slid her hand into mine.

"It'll be over before you know it," I replied with a grin as I put my hand on the small of her back. Her eyes widened, and I swallowed hard at the feel of her against me. She was all soft and curved, and it was hard for me to focus. Fuck, it was just hard for me in general. She was beautiful. Gorgeous, and she smelled like sin. Or maybe that was just floral perfume. I didn't know, but she was gorgeous. How was I supposed to focus when she was pressed up against me?

"Hopefully, the song will be over soon. I'm sorry. I don't mean to be a jerk, but I do have things to do for the wedding, and I'm not supposed to actually be around and in the spotlight like this."

I swallowed hard as the music turned into something softer, and we danced carefully.

"I should probably tell you then I shouldn't be in the spotlight either."

Her eyes narrowed even as her lips twitched. "Tell me I'm not dancing with a wedding crasher."

"Technically, I was invited. Just not by the wedding party."

She looked up at me, blinked. "You are with Roy then."

I frowned. "I don't know if *with Roy* is the right statement."

She laughed and it lit up her whole damn face. What the hell was with this connection? "You're here to watch Roy and to see what he does because you're thinking about buying something similar. To join the innkeepers and wedding venue circuit."

I couldn't stop staring at her mouth, so it took me a minute to catch up with her words. "I didn't realize he told you all that."

"Of course, Roy told me. We're about to have strangers at the wedding. I should have put it together beforehand, but I've been a little sidetracked. Busy day."

"It sure looks like it. The wedding looks fantastic, though."

"I hope so." She looked around, smiling softly.

"We worked hard on it. And the bride and groom are beautiful together."

I looked over at them as they swayed from side to side, not dancing, just the two of them holding one another off the dance floor. It was just the two of us on the dance floor. Alone. With all eyes on us.

I held back a frown at the thought, even with the warmth of the woman in my arms. "I don't know if I like being the center of attention. I won't be once we run the place."

She smiled softly at me, her eyes filled with understanding. "No, you won't be. And neither one of us should be here in the limelight now."

I grinned. "I won't tell if you won't."

"I think the cat's out of the bag on that one," she whispered, her eyes dancing with laughter. She smelled so good and felt fucking amazing against me. I wanted her. Just like that, I wanted her.

There was a connection there, I could feel it, and from the way that she swayed into me, even though I knew she didn't want to because she was working, I felt like maybe she felt it too. Or maybe that's just what I wanted. What I was dreaming about and imagining.

"You're a wedding planner then. But you don't work for Roy full-time."

"He told you that?"

"Seems like Roy likes talking about everyone in his circles to each other," I said with a laugh.

"Seems like. And I own my own business. It would be nice just to work for Roy, but Roy wasn't sure if he wanted a full-time wedding planner since he has an event planner on hand."

I nodded softly. "We're thinking along the lines of having both. Because my brother Elliot would be great at all the other planning that comes to the resort, and any minute details that would come about. However, wedding planning isn't something we've ever done before."

"And running an entire inn and business like this is?"

"You got me there, but I don't know if Elliot really wants to do that."

"So would you hire on a wedding planner ad hoc, or would you have one on full-time?"

"That's the discussion right now, and we're leaning towards full-time."

She grinned, and I couldn't help in joining her. "Sounds like you guys are planning well."

"If this weekend goes well, we sign on the dotted line on Monday."

Her eyes widened, even as my heart raced. I

didn't know if it was the thought that we'd be spending a shit-ton of money on Monday or that smile on her face.

Damn it, I didn't have time for this or complications, and yet I wanted her.

There was something seriously fucking wrong with me.

"Well, I think Roy said this would be a couple of hours away, so not exactly in my jurisdiction as it were, but I know some people. I'll make sure you get my card afterward."

"I see, you just want to give me your number?" I asked, teasing. I surprised myself by even saying it since that wasn't normally like me, but she just smiled at me and shook her head.

"For work, buddy. I *am* working."

The song began to shift to something else as people came out onto the dance floor, joining us, and I almost hated the interruption. But the connection didn't snap. It didn't go away. It was still there.

"That's our cue. It was lovely meeting you, Eli. And I will get you my card." She paused. "For work."

"Whatever you say. The wedding is gorgeous."

"Thank you, and I hope you sign on that dotted line on Monday. I don't know. I just have a good feeling."

So did I, but I didn't say it. At least not then.

I followed her off the dance floor, ready to see if she wanted a drink, even if she was working. I couldn't help it. Everett gave me a weird look, but I turned and kept my attention on the woman I couldn't keep my mind off.

That was when I noticed the man in the slick gray suit, fancy haircut, and wide smile on his face come up to her.

She stiffened for just a moment.

"Clint," she whispered as she pushed her honey-brown hair back from her face. Some of it had fallen from her bun and made her look far more disheveled than she was.

Clint. Well then. Either this guy was an ex, someone she didn't want to meet, or someone that was going to ruin any plans that I had.

"Baby. I talked it over with the bride, and well, you are amazing. I love you." He went down to one knee, and the bride started to squeal, clapped her hands as everybody started to murmur in hushed tones, either cheering or with wide eyes.

I looked at the man on one knee in front of the woman I swore I'd had a connection with, at her wide eyes, and held back a sigh.

Fuck.

I turned to see Everett there, his own eyes wide. "You know what, let's do this. Wilder Resorts. We can do this. The six of us. We'll figure it out."

My brother cleared his throat. "I know we will. And what about the girl?"

I held back a snort as we made our way through the crowd, people cheering around us. "Clearly not for me. I don't need a woman. We all know what happens when we let our guard down.

"Yeah. We do."

And with that, I left the wedding alongside my brother. The two of us ready to meet with the other four and plan the rest of our lives. We had shit to do. Things that were all Wilder and just for us.

And I pushed all thoughts of a wedding planner, a bright smile, and a connection that clearly hadn't been real out of my mind.

CHAPTER FOURTEEN

Alexis

I stood transfixed as my boyfriend of two years knelt in front of me in his Armani suit, and I just blinked. Mortification slid over me, embarrassment slamming into it.

"Clint," I whispered fiercely, wondering what the hell he could have been thinking. *This was someone else's wedding.*

Not only were public proposals tacky, but they were also the worst things in the history of all wedding planning. *You never proposed in public.* What if the person wanted to say no? What if things got weird? Because they were already really fucking weird.

I loved Clint. I truly did. I knew we were going to get married.

But how could he not know me well enough to understand that a public proposal at a wedding I was working at would not be a good idea? Why did he think that that would be a good idea?

"Baby. I love you. You plan all the weddings. You put everyone else's needs and happy ever afters in front of your own. Now, baby, it's time to plan your own happy ever after. To plan ours."

I just blinked at him, my mouth going dry. "Clint."

"I know you're looking at me like I've lost my damn mind. Maybe I have. But I love you. I've already talked to the bride and groom. You know I work with him."

"Oh. Right."

Why couldn't I say anything longer than a word or two? Why couldn't I focus or breathe? Why couldn't I do anything other than want to run away but unable to do so?

"I love you, Alexis. I want to spend the rest of my life with you. Here on the happiest days of two of my friends, they gave me permission to ask you to make me the happiest man on this earth." I looked over his shoulder sharply at the bride and groom as they held each other, tears flowing down the bride's cheeks. She gave me a thumbs-up and mimicked drinking tea, and I wanted to pass out. Over and away.

She had seen this in her tea leaves. Of course she had.

I looked to the right to see Emily rushing towards me, her mouth gaping open, her eyes wide.

I saw the look of *what the fuck* on her face, and it mirrored my own.

However, if I walked away, if I broke down and broke Clint's heart right here, I would be the bitch of all bitches. I would ruin this wedding and put a pall over everything. Nobody would ever want to hire me again. I would lose my job. Lose my sanity. I would lose everything.

This man, the love of my life, had proposed to me in the worst way possible for a wedding planner, but he seems so earnest about it.

I couldn't ruin this day for anyone.

I wanted this, I reminded myself. I wanted happiness.

Clint was mine. He was my forever.

We might as well start now and not ruin everything that I had worked towards along the way.

I lean down, and whispered, "Yes."

He beamed as he went to his feet and cheered, "She said yes!"

"Champagne for everybody!" The bride shouted out, and the room cheered, clapping each other on the back and laughing and taking photos. Clint cupped my face and kissed me softly.

"I knew you would love this. I knew this was perfect."

I looked at the man that I loved, at my fiancé, as he slid the ring onto my finger, a ring I didn't even notice because I couldn't breathe, and had to wonder if I had just made the biggest mistake of my life.

Want to see exactly how Eli and Alexis make it back to each other?

Read their romance in ONE WAY BACK TO ME!

ABOUT THE AUTHOR

Carrie Ann Ryan is the New York Times and USA Today bestselling author of contemporary, paranormal, and young adult romance. Her works include the Montgomery Ink, Redwood Pack, Fractured Connections, and Elements of Five series, which have sold over 3.0 million books worldwide. She started writing while in graduate school for her advanced degree in chemistry and hasn't stopped since. Carrie Ann has written over seventy-five novels and novellas with more in the works. When she's not losing herself in her emotional and action-packed worlds, she's reading as much as she can while wrangling her clowder of cats who have more followers than she does.

www.CarrieAnnRyan.com

Made in the USA
Middletown, DE
24 October 2024

63223260R00119